94

D0419071

THE ROMAN WORLD

First published in 1986 by Kingfisher Books Limited,
Elsley Court, 20-22 Great Titchfield Street,
London W1P 7AD

© Kingfisher Books Ltd 1986

British Library Cataloguing in Publication Data
Corbishley, M.C.
The Roman World (Kingfisher ancient history)
1. Rome—History—Juvenile literature
I. Title   II. Salariya, David   III. Willis, Shirley
IV. Biesty, Stephen
937   DG209

ISBN 0 86272 218 7

Edited by Kate Hayden and Anne Priestley
Designed by Nick Cannan
Picture research by Jackie Cookson
Phototypeset by Tradespools Ltd
Printed in Italy

The publishers wish to thank the following for
supplying photographs for this book:

8 Museum of London; 9 *top* Mauro Pucciarelli,
bottom ZEFA; 10 University of Cambridge,
Committee for Aerial Photography; 13 Mike
Corbishley; 16 Ashmolean Museum; 17 ZEFA; 19
Mansell Collection; 21 Mauro Pucciarelli; 23
Giraudon; 24, 30 Mansell Collection; 32/33 Mauro
Pucciarelli; 38 Sheridan Photo Library; 41 Mike
Corbishley; 43 S. Halliday and Laura Lushington; 44
Mike Corbishley; 45 C. M. Dixon; 47 The
Photosource; 50 Mike Corbishley; 55 Italian Ministry
of Defence; 54–55 RAPHO; 57 Michael Holford; 58
Naples National Museum; 62 Mike Corbishley; 63
Colchester and Essex Museum; 64 Mansell Collection;
66 Yorkshire Museum; 68 *top* University of
Newcastle-upon-Tyne, *bottom* Colchester and Essex
Museum; 69 *top left* Warburg Institute, University of
London, *top right* College of Ripon and St John; 71
The Manchester Museum; 73 *top* Mike Corbishley,
bottom Roger White; 79 Mike Corbishley; 81 SCALA;
82 Mauro Pucciarelli; 88 Yugoslav Tourist Office.

The publishers also wish to thank the following artists
for contributing to the book:

Stephen Biesty pp. 36–7, 52–3, 60–1, 69, 83–4;
Nick Cannan pp. 11, 18, 20, 39, 43, 48, 80;
Nick Harris pp. 65, 74, 83 (*bottom*), 76–7;
Kevin Maddison pp. 4, 6, 7, 14, 15, 19, 21, 28–9,
  34–5, 41, 44, 50, 51, 54, 57, 59, 62, 67, 70, 71,
  72, 75, 79, 81, 83 (*top*), 89;
Malcolm Porter pp. 7, 25, 31, 45;
David Salariya cover and pp. 26–7, 46, 56, 78;
Shirley Willis pp. 86–7.

Kingfisher History Library

THE ROMAN WORLD

Mike Corbishley

Kingfisher Books

CONTENTS

The Roman World

The Roman Peoples

Have you ever thought about the peoples who live in the United States of America? *Peoples* because the population of America is made up of many different races—Chinese, British, Jews, Russians, Italians and so on. Since the 17th century large numbers of people who wanted a new start in life have emigrated to America. Now people there can say "I am an American citizen—I belong here in the country of America" even though they, or their families, originally came from somewhere quite different.

In some ways America and Rome are similar. The lands you see marked on the map on the right were all part of the Roman Empire but the peoples in each country, or *province* to use the Roman name, were all different. All these people (and there were about 60 million of them) thought of themselves as Romans.

The idea of being Roman but coming from, say Aegyptus or Britannia, can be illustrated by a story which you may already know. Paul, a Jew from the province of Cilicia, became a Christian. After his preaching tours of the Mediterranean he was arrested in Jerusalem. The military commander ordered him to be whipped but Paul said to the officer in charge, "Is it lawful for you to whip a man who is a Roman citizen, and without a trial?". This was enough to stop the torture and the commander released Paul straight away.

The Latin Language

One of the things which helped join peoples together was a common language—like using English in North America or Russian, which is the main language of the peoples of the Soviet Union even though that country is made up of 15 different republics or states. Latin was the official language of the Roman World, even though people had their own language and dialects. You will come across many Latin words in this book, both in the examples from Roman writing and in the English itself because parts of our language come from Latin. Using an atlas, find out which modern countries make up the territory of the Roman World. How many modern names come from Roman ones?

Hadrian's Wall
This stone wall, with its forts and look-out points, was built by the Emperor Hadrian as a frontier in Britain. It stretched for 80 Roman miles (120 km).

Pont du Gard
This aqueduct *carried water to the Roman town of Nemausus (now Nîmes) in Gaul from a source 50 km away. Here it bridges the River Gardon.*

Road to Carthage
Roman roads were famous for being well-built on the most direct route. A messenger on a horse could travel about 75 km a day along them.

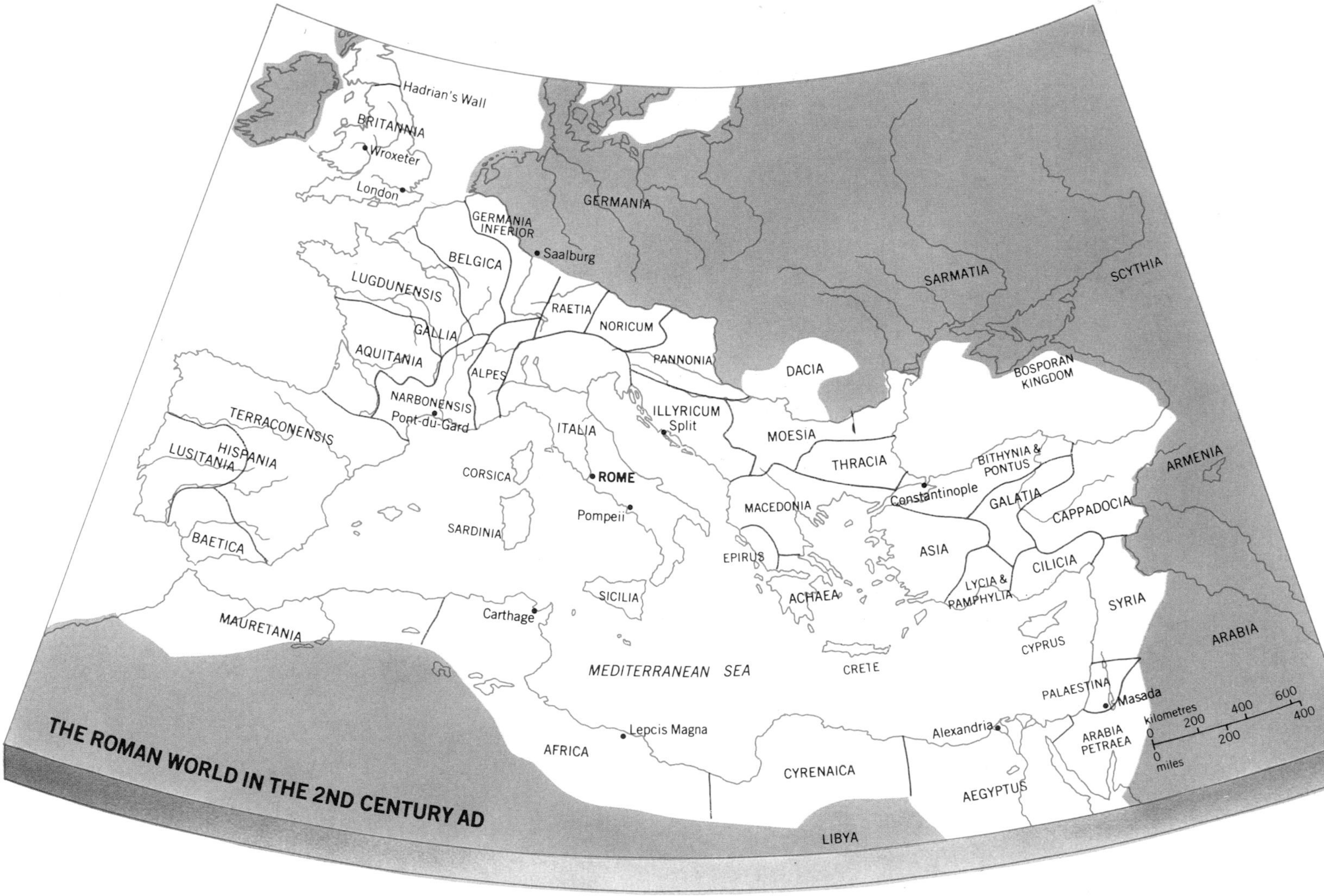
THE ROMAN WORLD IN THE 2ND CENTURY AD
Hadrian's Wall
BRITANNIA
Wroxeter
London
GERMANIA
GERMANIA INFERIOR
Saalburg
BELGICA
LUGDUNENSIS
GALLIA
AQUITANIA
RAETIA
NORICUM
PANNONIA
ALPES
NARBONENSIS
Pont-du-Gard
TERRACONENSIS
HISPANIA
LUSITANIA
BAETICA
CORSICA
SARDINIA
ITALIA
ROME
Pompeii
ILLYRICUM
Split
DACIA
MOESIA
THRACIA
SARMATIA
SCYTHIA
BOSPORAN KINGDOM
BITHYNIA & PONTUS
Constantinople
GALATIA
CAPPADOCIA
ARMENIA
MACEDONIA
EPIRUS
ACHAEA
ASIA
LYCIA & PAMPHYLIA
CILICIA
SYRIA
CYPRUS
ARABIA
SICILIA
Carthage
MAURETANIA
MEDITERRANEAN SEA
CRETE
PALAESTINA
Masada
ARABIA PETRAEA
Alexandria
AEGYPTUS
CYRENAICA
LIBYA
AFRICA
Lepcis Magna
kilometres
0
200
400
600
miles
0
200
400

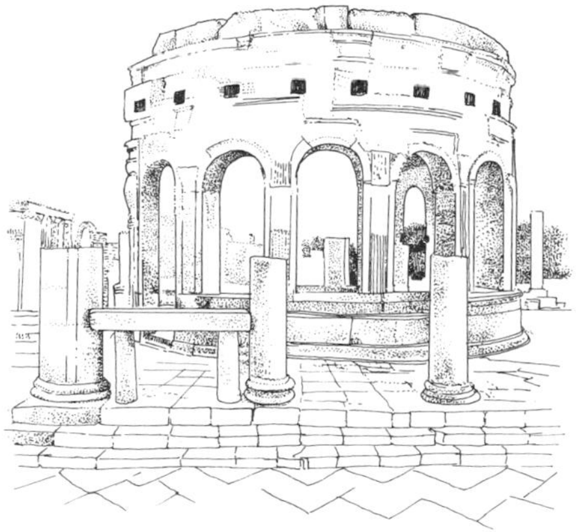

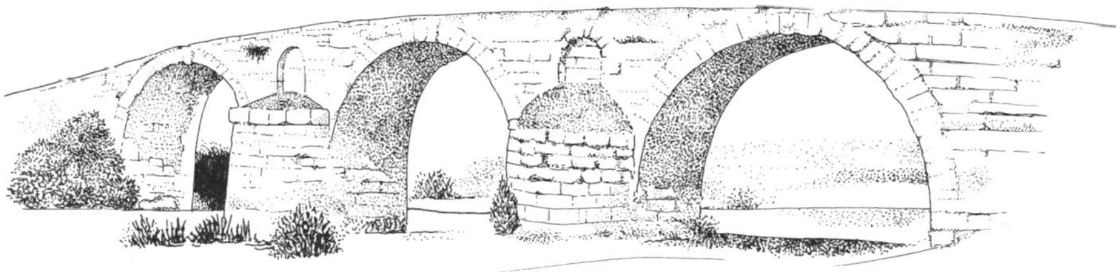

Market Building at Lepcis Magna
Above is one of two circular buildings, probably used by market officials. Traders had their stalls around in an enclosed and partly covered courtyard.

Theatre in Cyprus
The theatre below is in the Roman capital of Cyprus, Augusta (now called Paphos). Any decent sized Roman town in the provinces was expected to have a theatre.

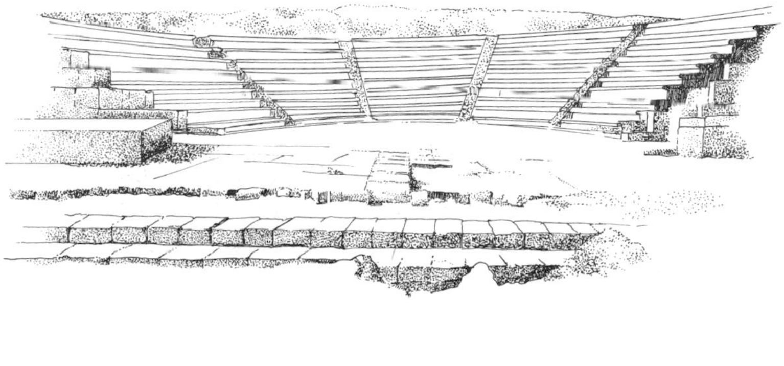

Bridge in Syria
The Romans were good engineers and builders. They knew how to construct arches to carry heavy weights in buildings or, as above, in a bridge over the River Afrin.

The Evidence

Roman Remains

Detective stories and films sometimes have the following words near the title: "The characters in this story are imaginary and bear no relation to any living person or actual happening." Well, this book is not like that at all. What you will read about the Romans is based on actual *evidence* and on actual *characters*. In the next few pages you will find out what sort of evidence there is of the Roman World. More examples of evidence occur all through the book.

Anyone who wants to investigate the past will soon find out that it's a bit like doing a jigsaw puzzle—but with a lot of the pieces missing! Why are there pieces missing? Why do some pieces survive? The reasons are complicated because it depends on a number of different circumstances in various parts of the world. Let's look at some examples.

Buildings Re-used

Many Roman towns continued to be used for centuries after the fall of the Roman Empire and are still occupied today. Roman buildings in some towns can still be seen, even though they are in ruins. The *forum* in Rome (see pages 36–7) is a good example of this. Some buildings were *adapted* or changed so that they could be used for something else. The amphitheatre at Luca (opposite) is an example and another is the temple in Rome called the Pantheon (see page 62) which was turned into a church. These buildings *survived* but most do not because they become too old and are knocked down to make way for new ones. The building materials (such as stone) might be re-used in the new buildings.

Another example of the survival of evidence is the way some *organic* materials (that is, things which have been alive at one time, such as wood or seeds) are preserved. The *papyrus* on page 12 survived because it was discovered buried in very dry conditions in Egypt. Remember that Egyptian mummies are usually well-preserved. Sometimes organic material is so badly burnt that it survives, like the loaves of bread at Pompeii on page 46.

Doing the Jigsaw

So, if you are doing a jigsaw puzzle, where do you start? The answer is at the edges—that is, gather up all the pieces you can identify and try to put them together. When you have done this you will then find that other pieces will fit. If your jigsaw puzzle is about the past, what do you do about the missing pieces? You use the other evidence about the Romans which you have collected and guess what the pieces *might* have been. Try it with a real jigsaw and you will find it works—provided there are not too many pieces missing!

The girl is carefully cleaning a mosaic floor from a house in the Roman town of Londinium (now London). The mosaic floor does not survive all in one piece. During medieval times holes for rubbish (the girl is in one of these) were cut through and destroyed part of the Roman building. The mosaic floor was protected because the house it was in was abandoned and over the centuries new buildings were constructed over the demolished remains of the old ones, raising the ground level. In places, modern London is 6 metres higher than Roman Londinium.

Above: Luca (now Lucca) in Etruria, northern Italy.

Below: Thysdrus (now El Djem, Tunisia) in the Roman province of Africa.

Extraordinary Survivals

Amphitheatres were originally built for 'games' where people and animals were cruelly killed. These huge oval-shaped buildings were put to different uses in the period after the Romans. The one above survives as part of the medieval Italian city of Lucca. You can see its shape even though the seats for the spectators are gone. People began to re-use the great structure and build houses there. The inside of the amphitheatre remains an open space. On the other hand, the one on the right survives in the desert and can be seen for miles around. It was built in AD 238 by the Emperor Gordian I. It has survived for two reasons. First, it was a good place for the people of the area to hide in from their enemies. Second, it was in an area where there were few towns so there was no need to re-use the stone to build with in later periods.

Looking for the Romans

Today a great many people walk along Hadrian's Wall in Britain, or join guided tours of the *forum* in Rome, or tramp breathlessly past the Roman fort and up the steep slope of Masada in Israel. How do we know they are all Roman? The answer is that people have been fascinated by the past for centuries now and have been busy investigating the remains on the ground and the writing which the Romans have left us.

The First Archaeologists

In Europe by the 18th century there were a number of *antiquaries,* as they were called, busy collecting information about old or antique remains. Many made careful, and extremely useful, records of what they saw. Here is a quotation from the 18th-century British antiquary, William Stukeley, writing about the Roman town which lies under modern Exeter:

"One arch of South-gate seems to be Roman. No doubt the walls of the city are upon Roman foundations for the most part, and great numbers of antiquities have been found here. In digging behind the guildhall in Pancras-lane, they found a great Roman pavement of little white square stones eight feet deep".

By the 19th century many antiquaries were turning to excavation because they were *curious* or fascinated with the past. Some still preferred to investigate what could be seen on the ground. William Hutton set off at the age of 78 to walk Hadrian's Wall in 1801 because he wished "to see the greatest of all curiosities left us by the Romans". Later he wrote and published a full description with detailed sketches of what he had seen.

This aerial photograph of part of the Roman town of Wroxeter, near Shrewsbury in Britain, shows the sort of evidence which crops can reveal about the past. You can pick out the modern evidence on the photograph quite easily—fields, roads and farm buildings.

THE EVIDENCE

Modern Fieldwork

Today, archaeologists make use of the investigations of the antiquaries but also need to search for evidence themselves. Fieldwork involves combing countryside and town for evidence of the Romans. The archaeologist can also be helped by a number of modern methods which were not available to antiquaries in the 18th and 19th centuries.

Aerial Photography

The most important of the archaeologist's scientific techniques is aerial photography. An antiquary called William Camden seems to have been the first, in 1586, to have spotted that crops growing in fields sometimes show up remains from the past, buried under the soil. These marks, called *crop-marks*, are usually impossible to see and understand at ground level but they become clear from the air, as the photograph on the left shows.

The reason why marks show is that the growth of a crop (such as wheat, barley or sugar-beet) is affected by what its roots are growing over. Ditches and holes which have been filled up with soil will help the crop grow stronger or taller. Plants growing above the foundations of a stone wall might not do very well.

Look carefully at the photograph on the left. Look first at the dark lines. Can you see two parallel lines running down the photograph? They are the filled-in ditches of a Roman fort. The crop here is growing strongly in good, deep soil. However, most of the marks you can see are white. The wide ones show where the Roman streets were and the thin ones the outlines of Roman houses. The crop here has suffered badly because its roots are in a thin layer of soil over stone walls.

After a very dry summer the marks often show up better. Crops over walls will suffer even more in drought but crops growing over ditches draw upon the damp soil buried far below the surface.

Roman Wroxeter

The Roman army of occupation in the province of Britain first came to a flat plain on the edge of the River Severn in about AD 48. A number of small camps were built at first and then a camp large enough for an entire *legion* (about 5500 men) was built here. Round about AD 90 the army finally pulled out and a town was established here which the Romans called Viroconium Cornoviorum— the town of the native tribe called the Cornovii.

Above: Fieldwalking in action. The rods, called ranging rods, are used by surveyors, architects and builders as well as archaeologists.
Right: Equipment includes tape measures, notebook and pencil, plastic bags and labels.

Fieldwalking

Fieldwalking is just what it sounds like—walking over fields! The idea is to make a careful collection of objects which have been brought to the surface by ploughing. The remains of buildings or places where people buried their rubbish will leave a scatter of evidence from the past.

To be really useful the collection of evidence must be carefully done. Here are the rules:

1 First, the field to be walked must be measured out and a map or plan made.

2 On the field itself you must know *exactly* where you are walking so that anything you find can be plotted on to the map of the field. The drawing above shows rods marking out the *grid* (just like graph paper). Each grid square is numbered on your plan.

3 The people in the drawing are picking up evidence from the surface—pottery, roof tiles, pieces of iron etc. Everything collected is put into plastic bags with labels which record exactly which grid square they came from. The label above shows the *code* for one particular square.

4 After the material has been collected it is cleaned and the code marked on.

5 Then the material is *analysed*—looked at closely—and divided into different categories (pottery or tile, for example). You can then work out where people were living in this area in the past.

6 Finally a report is written about the work and all the material (usually called *finds*) is stored in a local museum.

11

Writing and Excavation

We have seen in the previous pages how quite a lot of evidence of the Romans survives above ground for us to visit and that some can be detected in the soil by different methods. We are now going to look at ways of finding *detailed* information about the Romans. There are two sorts of evidence—*written* and *excavated* evidence.

Written Evidence

We know a great deal about the Romans from the books they wrote. History books tell us about great events and the people concerned. From letters we discover something about the public and private lives of Romans all over their world. There are plenty of other sorts of writing—plays, poems, reference works, recipe books, even official lists and accounts.

Here is one example, and you will be coming across many others in the book. This is part of a letter from the writer Plinius (usually called Pliny) to the Emperor Trajan. Pliny was appointed governor of the province of Bithynia in AD 101.

> "While I was making a tour of inspection of another part of the province, a huge fire in the city of Nicodemia destroyed many private houses and public buildings. It spread as far as it did for two reasons—because there was a strong wind blowing and because people just stood around watching it happen without doing anything. Anyway the city does not even have one pump, fire bucket or any fire-fighting equipment."

Only rarely, though, do the actual books written out by the Romans survive 2000 years later. How, then, can we still read so much of what was written during the Roman period? The answer is that a great deal of it was copied out by monks in medieval times.

Some examples of actual Roman writing do survive. Some books or letters written on papyrus have been found in the hot dry climate of Egypt. The fragment (left) is part of the writings of the poet Cornelius Gallus, who lived during the period of Caesar and Augustus. Papyrus was the Roman equivalent of paper, made from the stems of a water plant growing in the Mediterranean area but especially in Egypt.

Excavated Evidence

Now let's think about the other source of evidence—archaeological evidence—that is, actual remains. This evidence can be of all sorts of things. For example, of where people lived and worked or of the things they threw away or lost. Archaeologists are interested in all remains of the past—from the way a town was laid out to the tiniest piece of bone which might give us a clue to what a family had for lunch.

We have seen that only a few pieces of writing survive from the Roman period compared with the enormous amount that must have been written. This is also true of archaeological evidence—only part survives, so the story of the past has to be pieced together like a jigsaw puzzle. Archaeologists have to become skilled, just like detectives, in working out what happened from the evidence they can find.

Excavation is used when very detailed evidence has to be collected. On the right is a photograph of a recent excavation at the Roman town of Wroxeter in Britain. Although some walls of the *basilica* (meeting-place) being uncovered stand above ground, archaeologists have to dig for most of the evidence. The site was abandoned, and most of the walls were removed for building stone. The floors gradually became covered with soil, mainly washed down from the hill-slope above, and what had been the centre of a busy Roman town became ploughed fields.

The digging you can see in the photograph is only part of what archaeologists call excavation. Walls and floors, for example, have to be very carefully uncovered, often using little tools like trowels and brushes. Each area is numbered and all the 'finds' collected are given the same 'code' number, just as in fieldwalking.

Each part of the site (such as a wall or a floor) is drawn and photographed and notes are made about it. The drawings made are like maps, accurately measured. All the drawings, photographs and notes form part of the site record. How many of these archaeological 'operations' can you see in the photograph?

Before the Romans

The Etruscans

Now that we have seen something of the evidence for the world of the Romans we must begin to look at the Romans themselves. Why, then, begin with the Etruscans? The answer is that history is not a simple story. The Roman peoples did not appear out of nowhere wearing togas, speaking Latin and controlling vast areas of their world. To understand how the Roman state began we must look back a little in time to the Etruscans.

If you look at the map on page 23 you will see where in Italy the Etruscans lived—Etruria. But where did they come from? Some evidence suggests they originally came from the area the Romans called Asia. Most people, however, think that the Etruscan civilization gradually developed in the area north of Rome.

Although there is quite a lot of *archaeological* evidence for the Etruscans we are not able to use *written* evidence from the Etruscans themselves. Their language was no longer spoken after the 2nd century AD and only a few inscriptions have survived until the present day.

In the 7th century BC the Etruscans formed twelve states in their part of Italy. These states were independent but allied together. It was from these twelve states, with a city in each, that the Etruscans began to conquer various parts of Italy. They pushed out to the north and the south along the coast (including the area around Rome) as far as the Bay of Naples by the 6th century BC.

The wealth needed for the Etruscans to build elaborate painted tombs (see below and right) came from their agriculture, their industries and their trading. They grew olives and grapes, produced grain, which they traded, and bred horses. They were excellent metalworkers and potters. Their ships traded with the Phoenicians, the Carthaginians and the Greeks.

The Etruscans were also good architects and engineers—they planned out their cities with proper roads, aqueducts and sewage systems.

The Romans were hostile to the Etruscans, as we shall see later, but did acknowledge that they got some of their ideas from them. For example, they called one type of entrance hall or *atrium* (see page 72) in their houses, Etruscan. Julius Caesar said that the Romans "eagerly copied any good idea, whether it was from a friend or an enemy".

Scenes from Etruscan Tombs
Left and below: A funeral banquet with flute and lyre players from Tarquinii.
Top Right: Chariot racing from Clusium.
Middle right: Wrestlers from Tarquinii.
Bottom right: Fishermen from the Tomb of the Hunters and Fishermen from Tarquinii.

BEFORE THE ROMANS

Inside the Tombs

The Etruscans believed in a life after death and held ceremonies and made sacrifices to the dead. They hoped those who died would guard their houses from the 'other world'. They built special underground tombs which had steps down to the burial chamber and a great mound on top. A few bodies were cremated but the dead were usually buried in special chambers inside the tombs. There were always objects buried with the dead—vases, offerings of food, statues and jewellery, for example.

Paintings on the Walls

The most impressive thing about Etruscan tombs are the colourful paintings on the walls—and sometimes the ceilings too. Etruscan painters were clearly skilful. The various drawings here show ceremonies conducted for the dead person: there is an open-air banquet with dancers and musicians at which games and sports are played. The stack of large bowls between the wrestlers is probably the prize they are fighting for.

Tombs and Tomb Robbers

While many Etruscan tombs have been discovered, excavated properly and preserved for everyone to look at, a vast number have been plundered by modern treasure-hunters—called tombaroli or clandestini in Italy today.

Proper archaeological investigation usually involves a probe being inserted into the tomb mound. A miniature camera on the end of the probe photographs all the painted walls so that at least there is some record to study.

The Republic

Rome Founded

By the 7th century BC the area just south of where the city of Rome was later to stand, was occupied by a tribe called the *Latini*—the Latins (see map on page 23). They were farmers who lived in villages on hills which they could defend against neighbouring tribes. By the end of the 7th century their simple way of life was being influenced by trading with the Carthaginians and the Greeks. The Etruscans also moved into their area. The villages of the Latins became towns.

One of these towns, Rome, began in about 575 BC, founded by the Etruscans. The word *Roma* seems to have been an Etruscan name. However, the people of Rome were not all Etruscan. There were many Sabines and Latins—in fact the Latins were the strongest influence on the city. The city itself was built on seven hills called the Quirinal, Viminal, Esquiline, Caelian, Aventine, Palatine and Capitoline.

Rome was in a very important location. It was well protected by its hills and was able to use the River Tiber to reach the sea. This was an outlet for trade and a useful point to begin conquering the territory around.

Roman tradition tells us that the people of Rome were ruled by a king—called a *rex*. He could have come from any of the peoples who formed the population of the city. The Romans believed that their first king was Romulus who was said to have founded the city on April 21, 753 BC. His story is told opposite. In the following pages we shall see how Romulus' city was the beginnings of a vast empire.

Rome on Coins

You will often see Roman coins in museums. Watch out for abbreviations of words and see if you can work out what the coin 'says'. You can easily see the word ROMA—Latin for Rome—on this coin which was minted or made in 220 BC. Driving the four-horse chariot is Jupiter and with him Victory represented as a goddess with wings. The Latins, especially, worshipped Jupiter, the king of the gods.

Like many Roman coins this one contains a lot of information, if you can 'read' it. In the centre is a man wearing a toga—*part of the national dress. He is probably the man who was responsible for minting this coin in about 85 BC. His name is given in a shortened version—POST(umius) ALBIN(us). He has his arm outstretched to a standard, or sacred emblem, of the army. On top is the eagle—Rome's symbol of power. On his right are the* fasces *(see page 18).*

THE REPUBLIC

The Story of Romulus and Remus

Like the Greeks before them, the Romans loved stories—especially legends about gods and goddesses, famous heroes of the past and their own ancestors. The Romans wanted to trace the foundation of their city to the gods. They believed that the great warrior Aeneas, son of Aphrodite the Greek goddess of love and beauty, had made a long voyage across the Mediterranean Sea after his city, Troy, had been captured by the Greeks. He was said to have founded the city of Lavinium, a few miles south of the River Tiber. Many, many years later . . .

. . . a descendant of Aeneas, King Numitor, was driven out by his wicked brother Amulius. King Numitor's daughter Rhea had just given birth to twin sons—Romulus and Remus—and their father was the mighty god of war, Mars. Amulius ordered the babes to be thrown into the River Tiber so that they could not take over the kingdom, which they were entitled to.

However, as luck would have it, they were put into a basket to float away to their deaths and, landing high and dry on the bank, were suckled by a she-wolf who had heard the babes' cries. They were discovered by the shepherd of the royal flocks, Faustulus, who carried the boys home to be raised by his wife and himself.

The boys grew up strong and wild and later formed a band which attacked robbers and divided the loot among the poor shepherds. During one exploit Remus was captured and the twins were recognized by their grandfather King Numitor . . .

. . . All was now revealed and they helped their grandfather regain his throne. They went on to found a city of their own on the site of Rome but an argument flared up between the two brothers over who was to rule the city and Remus was killed.

Romulus, the first king of Rome, built a city for fugitives like himself but he had to steal wives for his desperate band from a neighbouring tribe, the Sabines. After reigning forty years he mysteriously disappeared in the darkness of a great storm and was worshipped by the Romans as the god Quirinus, named after one of the seven hills of Rome.

This bronze statue of the she-wolf which was supposed to have suckled Romulus and Remus was made by an Etruscan craftsman in the 6th century BC. The two twins are 'modern'—they were added in the early 16th century AD. You can see the statue today in the Capitoline Museum in Rome.

How the Republic Worked

After Romulus a number of other kings ruled. First, Numa Pompilius, Tullus Hostilius and Ancus Martius were kings from Latin tribes. Then, the people of Rome were ruled by Etruscan kings—Lucius Tarquinius Priscus, Servius Tullius and Lucius Tarquinius (who was nicknamed 'Tarquin the Proud'). They were not like some kings and queens today who are given power because they are next in line to the throne. Roman kings were chosen from a royal family or families. The king had a lot of power and to *symbolize* or show that power, officials carried the *fasces* in front of him. The *fasces* was a bundle of rods surrounding an axe, tied together with a red strap. The *fasces* symbolized the right of the kings to beat and execute the people if they had done wrong.

To make sure that the king did not have complete power the senate and assembly of the people had some say in who the king was and what he could do—especially in time of war. However, there is always a danger in allowing one person to hold power as the Romans found out:

"Then, after what King Tarquin the Proud did came to be hated by the people of Rome, we were all thoroughly fed up with being ruled by kings and the government was put in the hands of the consuls—officials elected each year."

From a speech by the Emperor Claudius in the 1st century AD.

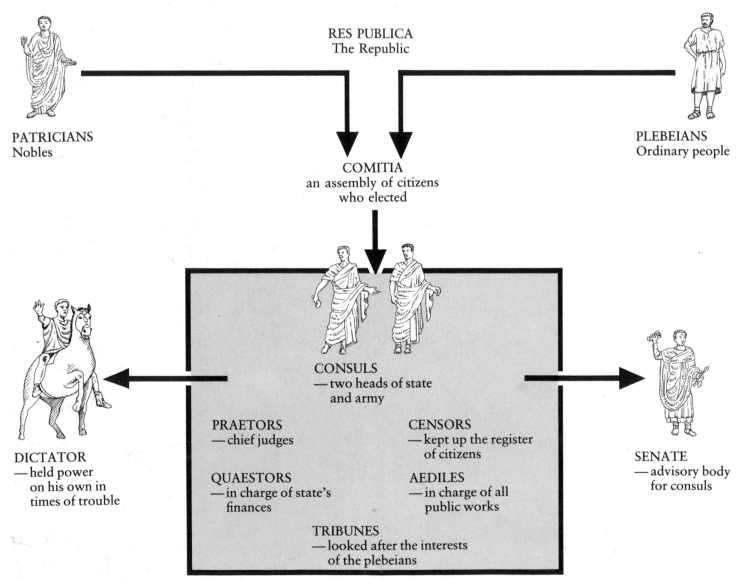

RES PUBLICA
The Republic

PATRICIANS
Nobles

PLEBEIANS
Ordinary people

COMITIA
an assembly of citizens
who elected

CONSULS
—two heads of state
and army

DICTATOR
—held power
on his own in
times of trouble

PRAETORS
—chief judges

QUAESTORS
—in charge of state's
finances

CENSORS
—kept up the register
of citizens

AEDILES
—in charge of all
public works

TRIBUNES
—looked after the interests
of the plebeians

SENATE
—advisory body
for consuls

THE REPUBLIC

A bronze statue by an Etruscan artist of an orator. Oratory—the art of arguing out points in public speeches in the law courts and in the senate—was considered so important that it became a major part of a boy's education.

Dates
Our yearly dates are based on the supposed date of the birth of Christ. The years before Christ (BC) are counted backwards—for example, Julius Caesar invaded Britain first in 55 BC, then again in 54 BC. From the birth of Christ the dates are counted forwards. AD stands for Anno Domini—'in the year of the Lord'. The Romans worked out their yearly dates from the foundation of the city of Rome or from a list of consuls elected each year.

According to Roman tradition the date for throwing out the kings and establishing the *respublica*—the republic—was 509 BC. A republic is a type of state where those who govern are elected by the people of the state. Those allowed to vote in elections are called citizens and in Rome were divided into two classes at first—Patricians and Plebeians. In the 2nd century BC another class emerged called the Equites—rich businessmen who did not come from any of the noble families of the patrician class. Citizens from all classes could become officials in the government although a plebeian was not allowed to become a consul or a dictator. However, as officials were not paid, only the wealthy tended to become politicians.

In many countries today the government is elected for a particular time, for example five years. Roman officials were elected for a shorter time. The most important were the two *consuls* who served for one year only. They had to agree with each other before they could act.

The Romans, then, established a democracy where citizens voted in their government. Many people, though, were not allowed to vote—all women, for example. Eventually the rich and powerful destroyed this democratic republic and established a new rule by one man—this time calling him an emperor not a king.

A scene in the senate house or curia. Part of the government was a group of elders, called senators, who were really there to advise the consuls. Even though the senate was supposed just to offer advice, the senators had a lot of authority. Senatus consulto—by command of the senate—was abbreviated to SC on many coins.

The Army and Navy

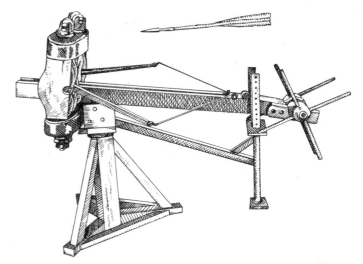

A Citizen Army

To become as powerful a people as they did (look again at the map on page 7) the Romans needed a large and well-trained army. All Roman citizens between the ages of 17 and 46 who owned property could be called up for service in the army or the navy. The heads of state, the two consuls, appointed *tribunes* to enrol free citizens, not slaves, into the various military units.

The Legion

Soldiers were organized into a number of *legiones*—legions. Each legion normally contained about 4200 men but sometimes this dropped to about 3000 after a campaign. It could also be increased to about 5000 if needed. Each legion had its own number and name. For example, one of the legions which invaded Britain in AD 43 under the Emperor Claudius was *XX* (The Twentieth) *Valeria Victrix*.

The Roman legion was divided into smaller units just as army regiments are today. Each legion was commanded by six tribunes, who took their orders from a consul, and was divided into 30 companies called *manipuli*. Each maniple was divided into two *centuriae*, literally units of 100 men. Each century was commanded by an experienced soldier called a *centurion* who had a second-in-command called an *optio*. There were also a standard-bearer, a trumpeter and a commander for guard-duty in each century.

On the left, the Roman legionary foot soldier of the Republic; on the right, two types of aquila *or eagle-standard of the Roman legions and a* signum *or standard of a* centuria *of a legion.*

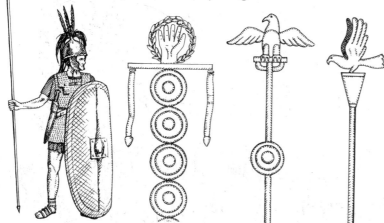

"The Roman legion is victorious because of its number of soldiers and the types of war machines it uses. It is equipped with ballistas—hurling machines—which can pierce body armour and shields." (Vegetius, writing in the 4th century AD.) The ballista *fired short iron-tipped bolts. The other main artillery weapon was the* onager—*a great stone hurling machine. For siege warfare the Romans used battering rams and huge siege towers.*

Battle Ranks

In battle the army was arranged in three lines. First came the *hastati* who were the strongest young men of the army. Next were the *principes* who were older citizens. Last came the *triarii* who were the most experienced soldiers. The poorest citizens would form a lightly-armed band called the *velites*. The richest citizens, who could afford a horse as well as weapons, provided the cavalry—usually about 300 for each legion.

The legionary soldiers used their long spears first against the enemy, then fought at close hand with their swords, daggers and shields—though usually in formation and under the strict command of the centurions. The standards were used like flags to rally the men to their own units to allow the commanders to reform the ranks. The cavalry squadrons would often sweep round on the wings to harass the enemy.

The Navy

"When the Romans saw that the war against the Carthaginians was dragging on, they decided for the first time to build ships, but their shipwrights were completely unused to building warships. However, one Carthaginian warship ran aground and into the hands of the Romans. They used this ship as a model to build their entire fleet."

Polybius, 2nd century BC.

It may seem extraordinary that such a powerful state had no fleet until the first war with Carthage in 264 BC (see page 24) but all Rome's wars up to then had been with land forces in Italy.

Even when ships were built they were often used as floating fighting platforms. The first move in a sea battle was to try to ram the enemy's ships so that they might sink. Look at the drawing on the right. This is the *prow* or front of a warship. Just below and in front of the crocodile is the under-water ram. If this did not work then a large ramp could be lowered on to the enemy's ship and the marines could rush across and fight as if they were on land.

The standard size Roman warship, which had 300 rowers and 120 marines (all free citizens) was called a *quinquereme*. The Latin word *quinque* means five and a quinquereme had three banks of oars on both sides of the ship. The top two banks had two men per oar, the bottom one had one oarsman—so, ranks of five rowers.

Professional Armed Forces

Later in the Republic the organization of the army and navy changed. Men volunteered to join up as legionaries, marines and oarsmen. They were paid for a long period of service. A legionary soldier would serve for 20 years and a seaman 26 years. Some served much longer—one centurion called Petronius Fortunatus chose to spend 50 years in the Roman army.

Above: This is part of a sculpture from the temple of the goddess Fortuna at Praeneste, near Rome. It probably commemorates the victory of Augustus, at the end of the republic, over Antony and Cleopatra.

Below: A painting from Pompeii of two warships at full speed. Notice the marines on deck with their shields and long spears.

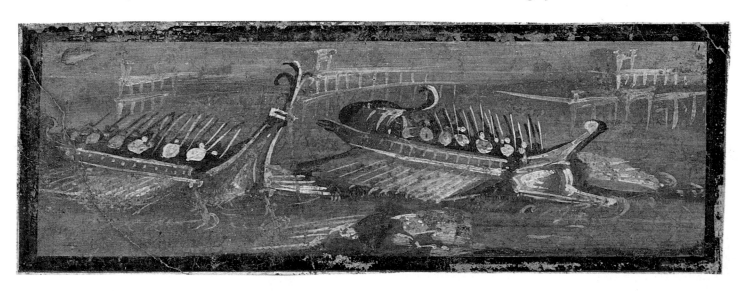

Threats to Rome

War, war, war! The Latin people in Rome and the area around seem to have been almost constantly at war in the early years of the Roman state. The map opposite shows the numbers of tribes which surrounded Rome itself. First of all the Latins had to deal with the Sabines, the Aequi and the Volsci. The Sabines lived to the north-east of Rome in villages in mountain valleys. Rome finally overcame them in 449 BC. The Aequi were, by Roman standards, rather primitive people, who lived in the mountain areas of central Italy. The Volsci, by about 500 BC, had established themselves around Rome. However, they were defeated by 304 BC.

In addition to these peoples, the Romans had to deal with those Etruscans living in the city of Veii about 19 km north of Rome. Veii was a rich and important town and resisted Roman attempts to conquer it for some time but it too fell to them by 396 BC.

The next enemies of Rome proved more of a problem to overcome. Celtic tribes called Gauls crossed the Alps in about 400 BC and moved south into Italy to find new land. We learn something about them from the historian Polybius:

"They lived in villages without defensive walls around them and spent their time in war or farming. Their only possessions were cattle and gold because this is what they could carry about with them."

The Gauls and the Wide-awake Geese

We know from other evidence that the Gauls were fine metalworkers and were brave, even reckless, in battle. They roamed the countryside in bands searching for loot and a good fight. In 390 BC a band of Gauls reached Rome. Most of the people of the city fled and the Gauls laid siege to one of the high points in the city which the Romans called the Capitol Hill. The Gauls tried to reach the top of the hill at dead of night. Those Romans who had taken refuge in the temples and other buildings on the hill were asleep ...

"One by one the Gauls pulled themselves up the side of the hill and reached the top. They were so silent that not even the guard dogs were woken up ... but the Gauls could not escape the notice of the geese, which were sacred to the goddess Juno. These geese saved the Romans by their cackling and the flapping of their wings."

Livy's History of Rome.

"*The greatest defeat of the day was caused by the unstoppable force of the elephants of King Pyrrhus.*" *This is part of an account by the historian Plutarch of a battle in 280 BC against the Greeks. The Romans lost to Pyrrhus who had brought with him twenty elephants like the one on the left. They were trained to charge at the enemy and sometimes carried a protected box on their backs, as here. This elephant has obviously charged and picked up an unfortunate warrior.*

THE REPUBLIC

Unfortunately the Gauls were not easily persuaded to leave Italy. In the end the Romans had to give them a large sum of gold to leave the country. Once the Romans had dealt with the Gauls they had to begin all over again with the Aequi, Volsci and Etruscans, and then deal with a new threat from the Osci.

A New Enemy—the Samnites

However, a new, even greater threat to the Republic of Rome appeared. The Samnites were a warlike group of peoples who lived in villages. They came together to fight the Romans so that they could win new territory for themselves. The Samnites were a serious threat to Rome because they had as many warriors as the Romans and were extremely well armed. There were three phases of war with the Samnites, beginning in 343 BC and finishing in Samnite defeat in 290 BC.

Even after all these wars the historian Livy could still write, "Our war with the Samnites was followed by a war with Pyrrhus and then followed by the war with Carthage." The Romans had gained control of the whole of Italy only to be faced with a greater threat—the Carthaginians.

Right: A heavily armed Samnite warrior. You can see how well he is protected— with chest and leg armour. He should also carry a spear and a shield. The Romans thought that the Samnites' weapons were better than their own and copied the idea of a long rectangular shield (called a scutum) from them.

Italy in the 6th century BC was populated by a number of different tribes—all with different languages and different ways of life. They were all a threat to the foundation of the Republic of Rome. Gradually, though, all the peoples on this map became part of the Roman state—whether they liked it or not!

Greek settlements
Carthaginian settlements

CELTS
RAETI
VENETI
CARNI
EUGANEI
LIGURES
ETRUSCANS
•Felsina
PICENI
UMBRIA
ILLYRIANS
Cortona•
SABINES
Vulci•
AEQUI
CORSI
Tarquinii•
•Rome MARSI IAPYGES
Alalia
Caere•
VOLSCI SAMNITES
LATINS
Olbia•
Cumae•
Capua•
OSCI
Metapontum
SARDI
Paestum•
•Tarentum
•Siris
•Sybaris
•Croton
ELYMI
•Himera SICULI
•Locri
Selinus•
SICANI
•Catania
Agrigentum•
Gela•
•Syracuse
Carthage•

Hannibal—Enemy of Rome

Hannibal

"Hamilcar was about to cross to Spain with his army and was making sacrifices. Hannibal, then about nine years old, was childishly teasing his father to take him too. His father, still angry at the loss of Sicily and Sardinia, led him to the altar and made him swear to be the enemy of Rome as soon as he was able."

"Many soldiers often saw Hannibal wrapped in a military cloak sleeping on the ground among the camp's guards. The clothes he wore were nothing out of the ordinary. He was the best among the foot and horse soldiers—first into battle and the last to leave."

The historian Livy.

After defeating most of the other tribes in Italy itself, the Romans had become what we would call today a world power. There was bound to be a conflict between Rome and other powerful countries in the Mediterranean area. The first to challenge Rome at this time were the Carthaginians whose capital was in North Africa.

Carthage had been established by a sea-faring, trading people called the Phoenicians from the Syrian coast. As you can see from the map on page 23, Carthage extended her territory beyond the African coast to the north of Sicily. Once the Romans had overcome the Greeks they had to deal with Carthage—also a world power.

Rome and Carthage at War

The first war with Carthage began in 264 BC and lasted for 23 years. Carthage moved from the south-west tip of Sicily and occupied the port of Messana—the nearest town to mainland Italy. The Romans sent two legions of soldiers to Messana, defeated the Carthaginian force and occupied the port. From a fight over one town in Sicily a full-scale war broke out. The Romans had to build a fleet of 120 ships, then later another of 200 ships, to combat the Carthaginian navy.

During this war the Romans occupied Corsica and Sardinia as well as driving the Carthaginians out of Sicily. Besides their defeat in battle the Carthaginians had to pay Rome a huge fine in silver as compensation for Roman losses.

Enter Hannibal

In the final stages of this first war the Carthaginian commander-in-chief had been Hamilcar Barca. In 237 BC, after the war with Rome, he led Carthaginian forces into Spain to defend the settlements already established there and to win new territory. Spain was very useful to Carthage because it supplied many goods—silver, copper, iron, food and fish.

Hamilcar's son Hannibal, then 25 years old, took over the command of the Carthaginian forces in Spain in 221 BC. By this time the Romans had begun to be worried by the Carthaginian forces close to their borders. First the Romans tried to talk rather than fight, but without success.

Eventually Hannibal besieged Saguntum on the coast of Spain. This town had a treaty with Rome and so war broke out again between these two world powers. The Romans sent two forces against Carthage—one to Africa and the other to Massilia (now Marseilles) to fight Hannibal. Hannibal outwitted the Romans by marching to Italy across the Alps. His army was huge—about 40,000 men and 37 elephants. Many of his soldiers died on that difficult journey across the Alps to Italy. There were only 26,000 men and about 12 elephants left when they arrived.

Across the Alps

Hannibal raised a new army (50,000 in all) in Italy—buying the services of Celtic warriors—and began to rage through the heart of the Roman state. The Romans were defeated in several major battles—at Lake Trasimene in 217 BC and then at Cannae the following year. Eventually a new young commander-in-chief of the Roman forces, called Publius Cornelius Scipio, was appointed. He managed to defeat one of Hannibal's armies in Italy. Scipio then took a large force across to Africa to attack Carthage itself. Hannibal was recalled to Carthage and in 202 BC Scipio defeated his army at Zama. Carthage lost all its territory this time as well as paying another huge fine. Hannibal himself escaped but eventually committed suicide in 183 BC to avoid being taken by the Romans.

Even after the death of Hannibal the Carthaginians did not accept rule from Rome. A third war began in 149 BC and ended in 146 with Scipio besieging Carthage, making the 50,000 people who survived slaves and completely destroying the city. What had once been Carthaginian territory became the new Roman province of Africa.

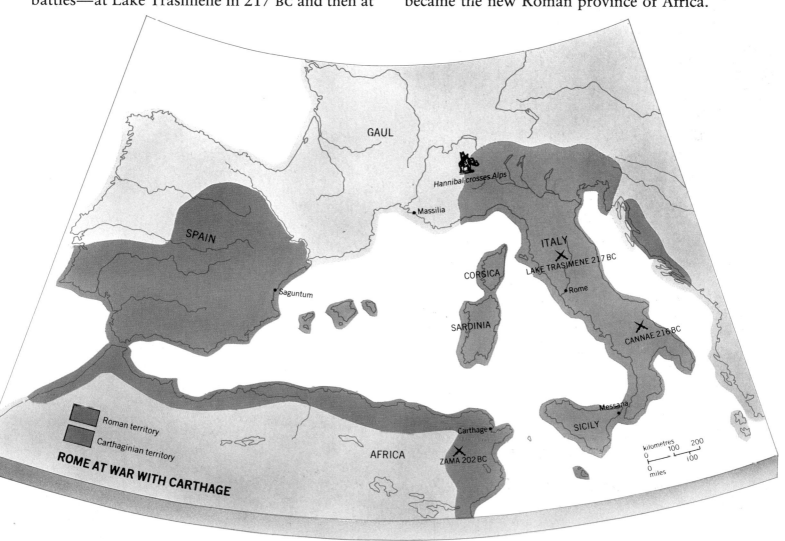

ROME AT WAR WITH CARTHAGE

"After nine days' climb Hannibal's army reached the snow-covered summit of the pass over the Alps—all the time being attacked by the mountain tribes. However, when the enemy now attacked the column the elephants were of great use to the Carthaginians. The enemy were so terrified of the animals' strange appearance that they dared not come anywhere near them."

Polybius, the historian.

Changes in the Republic

Even after the defeat of the Carthaginians, the Romans could not settle down to govern their new territories in peace. The Greeks were threatened by Macedonia and asked the Romans to help. The Romans declared war on King Philip V of Macedonia. He was finally defeated in 196 BC but the Romans went on to war against King Antiochus III of Syria who had extended his empire and moved into Thracia.

The campaign against foreign peoples—especially in or close to Italy—brought about two problems. One was that many people who were included in the Roman state simply did not want to be Roman and trouble often arose between an 'ally' and Rome itself. The other problem was that during these campaigns Rome had acquired a lot of land. It gave or let this to rich farmers who formed it into huge ranch-style estates. Poor farmers often had land taken away from them and farmworkers were gradually replaced by slave labour from the foreign wars. In other words, there were more and more people becoming unemployed and poor. Many people left the countryside and settled in towns, especially Rome, and then had to be fed by the government.

Land Reform

One man more than any other at this time saw that this was wrong and that, if nothing was done about it, it would cause trouble and uprisings against the government. This man was Tiberius Gracchus who became a *tribune* (see page 18) in 133 BC. He proposed a new law which gave much of the new land acquired by Rome to farmers in small plots. The farmers then paid a small rent to the state. A special commission was set up, including Gracchus himself, to make sure that the

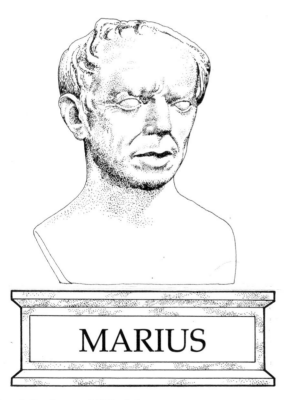

MARIUS

Gaius Marius   157–86 BC
As a politician Marius tried to win support from both the ordinary people and the senate. When civil war broke out with Sulla, Marius occupied Rome and murdered all his enemies. He appointed himself consul for the seventh time in 86 BC but died 18 days after taking up office.

SULLA

Lucius Cornelius Sulla   138–78 BC
Sulla brought about civil war in 83 BC when he marched on Rome at the head of his army to overthrow the government which had declared him a 'public enemy'. On his victory he declared himself dictator. It was really the ambitions and actions of Sulla and Marius which brought about the end of republican government in Rome.

new scheme worked. Although the law was passed there was naturally great opposition to it from those wealthy Romans who stood to lose their huge estates. In fact opposition was so fierce that they had Gracchus murdered.

Tiberius Gracchus' reforms were taken up by his younger brother Gaius. In 124 BC he was elected a tribune and re-elected the following year. During his period of office he saw various laws passed which helped the poor. One provided cheaper bread for Rome's poor. He also took some power away from the wealthy noble class and gave it to the *equites*—the business class of people. When he tried to be elected for a third time he too was hunted down. He had a slave stab him to death to avoid being captured but 3000 of his followers were arrested and executed.

Political Parties

"In the Roman state there have always been two groups of people eager to take part in, and be the leaders of, public life. One group wished to be known as *populares*, the other *optimates*."

Cicero.

Today we would call these groups that took part in public life political parties, although they were not quite the same. The *optimates* were really a group of the very wealthy who wanted to keep the wealth and power they had. This group tried to make sure that only those with their ideas got the important political posts in the government of Rome. The *optimates* strongly supported the idea of government through the senate.

On the other hand, the *populares* got their support from the ordinary working (or unemployed) people. They were also supported by some of the equites who wanted the power held by the nobility and the senate. It was the struggle between the supporters of these two opposing groups that led to trouble, civil wars and eventually the establishment of dictators and emperors.

CICERO

Marcus Tullius Cicero   106–43 BC
Cicero was the best of the Roman orators (public speakers). As a lawyer he was famous for his speeches against the terrible governor of Sicily, Verres, who had stolen from and murdered many of the inhabitants. Cicero fought with Pompey in the civil war against Julius Caesar, for which he was eventually put to death by Octavian.

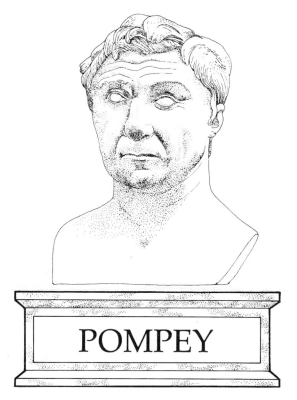

POMPEY

Gnaeus Pompeius   106–48 BC
Pompeius—Pompey—fought with Sulla in the civil war against Marius and added Magnus ('The Great') to his name in 81 BC after victory in Africa. He governed Rome with Julius Caesar and Marcus Crassus but later took the side of the senate against Caesar in the civil war. After defeat by Caesar's troops he was murdered in Egypt.

Julius Caesar

Roman records tell us that Julius Caesar was born between 102 and 100 BC. He, however, declared that he was descended from the gods. Whatever the truth of his godlike connections he was certainly born into an important Roman family of the *patrician* class. Through his aunt Julia's marriage he was a nephew of Marius. This connection with Marius brought him into conflict with Sulla who tried his best to kill off the young Caesar. His upbringing and education were quite normal for someone born into the aristocracy of Rome and by the time he was twenty he was serving with the army in Asia and Cilicia.

A Political Career

In 73 BC he was elected to the college of priests. He served as a *quaestor* in Spain; as an *aedile* he put on magnificent games in Rome; he was elected the head of the college of priests—*pontifex maximus;* he served as *praetor* and then went back to Spain as its governor *propraetor*. In Spain he campaigned against a tribe called the Lusitani, so adding more territory to the Roman state. In 60 BC, he was elected *consul*.

After his consulship he was able to choose the province he wanted to govern. In 58 BC he took on provinces in northern Italy and in Gaul and campaigned against the peoples there, in Germany and in Britain. In ten years, between 59 and 49 BC, he conquered a vast new area for the Roman state. No wonder Cicero praised him in the senate:

"Before, members of the senate, we only had a route through Gaul. All the other territories were occupied by peoples who were either hostile to us or could not be trusted. Some were unknown, savage, uncivilized or war-like. Caesar has fought very successfully against the fiercest of peoples in great battles and made them part of the Roman state."

Civil War

At the close of Caesar's term of office, Pompey was jealous of his great power and popularity and persuaded the senate to order him to disband his army. Caesar refused and war broke out between them—a civil war with Romans fighting Romans. You can follow the course of this war on the map on the right.

Julius Caesar is shown in this statue as a general. The writer Suetonius said that he was " . . . a bit of a dandy. He always kept his hair carefully trimmed and used to comb his few hairs forward to cover his baldness."

THE REPUBLIC

49 BC: By crossing the *River Rubicon* between his province and Italy itself Caesar declared war on the senate.

Caesar's army pursues Pompey's to *Brundisium* but hasn't enough ships to follow him to Greece.

Caesar decides to attack that part of Pompey's forces in Spain, defeating them at *Ilerda*.

48 BC: Caesar now pursues Pompey to Greece and, after a setback, defeats his forces at *Pharsalus*.

Pompey flees to *Alexandria* in Egypt to help Cleopatra in the war against her brother Ptolemy.

47 BC: Caesar takes his army back to Italy via Bithynia where he defeats King Pharnaces, an ally of Pompey, near *Zela*. The victory was so easy that Caesar sent a message to the senate simply saying, *"Veni, vidi, vici"*—*"I came, I saw, I conquered"*.

46 BC: Crossing to North Africa Caesar defeats forces led by Pompey's ally Cato at *Thapsus*.

45 BC: Finally Caesar defeats the remains of the army led by Pompey's son at *Munda* in Spain.

Caesar the Dictator

Julius Caesar was now in complete control of the government and armies of Rome. He eventually became 'dictator for life' in 44 BC. It was obvious that Caesar wanted to see an end to any form of republican government and wanted the supreme title of *rex*—king.

Death on the Ides of March

The aristocracy in Rome, led by Marcus Brutus and Gaius Cassius, decided to assassinate him. Caesar ignored all warnings from his friends, the utterings of the prophets and the 'signs' from the gods that he would die on the Ides of March. When he entered the Senate House on the Ides—March 15, 44 BC—he was surrounded by the conspirators and stabbed to death.

With Caesar's death the Republic finally came to an end because, as we shall see on the next page, his adopted son and successor Octavius became the ruler of Rome—but not without a struggle.

THE RISE OF JULIUS CAESAR

Britain invaded 55 and 54 BC.

Conquest of Gaul 58–52 BC.

Campaign in 61 BC against the Lusitani

Served in Spain 68 BC.

R. Rubicon

ILERDA

ROME

BRUNDISIUM

ZELA

PHARSALUS

Served with the army 81–78 BC.

75–74 BC studied on Rhodes.

MUNDA

THAPSUS

ALEXANDRIA

conquests of Caesar

approximate extent of Roman territory at Caesar's death, 44 BC

kilometres 0 200 400 600

miles 0 200 400

The Empire

Above: "Augustus was extremely handsome even when he was old but cared nothing for the way he looked. For example, he cared so little about his hair that, to save time, he would have two or three barbers working at the same time. While they were cutting his hair or giving him a shave he would be reading or writing something."

Suetonius, writing in the 2nd century AD. *Octavianus was given the title* Augustus—*meaning a person to be respected—by the senate in 27* BC.

End of the Republic

The murderers of the dictator Julius Caesar perhaps thought that on his death the old republic would be re-established. They were wrong. A number of powerful men were waiting to seize power for themselves, as Caesar had done. Among them were two who had been close friends and allies of Caesar. One was Marcus Antonius (we call him Mark Antony) who delivered a great speech at Caesar's funeral, stirring up the Romans against the murderers. The other was Gaius Octavius, Caesar's adopted son.

Octavius was related to Julius Caesar through his mother. She was the niece of Caesar. His father was a member of the *equites* class who had been a governor of the province of Macedonia. His father died when he was four and he was brought up by his mother but had always had Caesar caring for him. Julius Caesar adopted him officially as his heir and he became known as Gaius Julius Caesar Octavianus.

At the time of Caesar's murder, Octavianus was studying in Greece. He hurried back to Italy to avenge his adoptive father's death. At first he fought against Antony as the two men struggled for power. Later they joined forces against Brutus and Cassius whom they defeated. Then, once again, the two men struggled against each other for power. They divided the Roman world between them—Antony taking the East and Octavianus the West.

Left: Augustus is pictured here at the altar to the gods of the home. As emperor of the Roman state he acted like the head of a family making sacrifices to the gods on behalf of his people— the people of Rome. Here Augustus is an augur—*that is, he tried to see into the future by looking for signs from the gods. One way of doing it, shown here, was to observe the way chickens ate. It was thought to be a very good sign (or omen) if they dropped some food from their beaks.*

This marble statue shows Augustus at the age of about 45 wearing the full uniform of a Roman general. Notice in particular his decorative breast plate. It shows a Roman standard being handed back to a commander, which refers to the victory of Augustus over the Parthians. Above this scene (just below Augustus' neck) is Apollo, the sun god, with the chariot of the sun. Augustus thought of Apollo as his special protecting god.

War again

Antony had his base in Alexandria in Egypt and was in love with Cleopatra. He allowed Cleopatra and her son Caesarion (whose father was actually Julius Caesar) to be proclaimed as joint rulers of Egypt and Cyprus. Antony's three young children by Cleopatra were to govern various parts of the eastern Roman world. Antony had declared himself king of the east without actually taking on the title of *rex*.

Neither Octavianus nor the senate could allow this splitting of the Roman state and war was declared against Cleopatra in 31 BC. The final battle between Antony and Octavianus took place at Actium in Greece. Octavianus won and Antony and Cleopatra both committed suicide; he stabbed himself and died in her arms; she later committed suicide by allowing an asp (a snake) to bite her.

Octavianus declared peace throughout the Roman world on January 11, 29 BC. The Roman people had had fifteen years of unrest and civil war. All the men who had struggled for power before and after Caesar's death were gone—apart from Octavianus. From now on there was no more Roman Republic—it had become a state ruled by one man. Octavianus had made it an Empire and himself the emperor.

The Emperors

Augustus

"I waged many wars throughout the whole world by land and by sea ... I have been given many triumphs ... I have been consul thirteen times and have been a senator forty years. I repaired the aqueducts which were falling into ruin ... I repaired eighty-two temples in Rome ... I gave three gladiatorial shows at which 10,000 fought ... I restored peace throughout Gaul, Spain, Germany and in many other places. I added Egypt to the empire of the Roman people. The entire Roman people gave me the title of *Pater Patriae* [Father of the Country]."

Just before he died in AD 14 at the age of 76 the Emperor Augustus left a number of personal papers and documents to be stored away in the official library. Among them was one called *Res Gestae Divi Augusti*—the Works of the Divine Augustus, part of which is quoted above. During his long reign he had achieved an enormous amount. Perhaps the most important was a period of over thirty years when the Roman people were not at war with each other. One of the main reasons for this was that Augustus was very careful to make the senate feel that the idea of the Roman Republic still lived on. Officials, such as consuls, were still voted in.

However, Augustus was equally careful that the right people were voted in and that governors of provinces (who controlled large numbers of troops) were chosen by him. In fact Egypt, which Augustus mentions above, remained his own personal property and a law was passed forbidding any senator from entering the country without his permission.

Another great achievement of Augustus was the rebuilding of the city of Rome. The writer Suetonius records that Augustus boasted, "I found Rome built of sun-dried bricks. I leave her covered in marble". Augustus built a new *forum* and repaired temples, theatres, roads and bridges.

Although Augustus often talked about "restoring the Republic" he never did and his reign made it easy for the Romans to accept rule by emperors for the next six centuries. Augustus was considered a 'good' emperor but many of those emperors who followed him were not. Some were clearly mad, like Caligula and several spent all the money belonging to the state on themselves.

LIVIA

Livia   54 BC–AD 29
Livia was born Livia Drusilla and was originally married to Tiberius Claudius Nero. He divorced her so that she could marry Augustus in 38 BC even though she had a son Tiberius (later emperor) and was pregnant at the time. Augustus loved her dearly and she had a strong influence on him throughout his reign. After Augustus' death when the senate declared him a god, she became his priestess and was known as Julia Augusta. She remained a powerful member of the 'royal family' even after Augustus' death.

An Emperor's Titles

Emperors had a number of titles which they used in public announcements or on inscriptions or coins. Augustus adopted the word *Caesar* from his 'father' Julius Caesar. The word, then, stood for Emperor. The modern words for ruler, *Kaiser* (German) and *Czar* (Russian), come from Caesar. The word Augustus also became a word for Emperor. The word Emperor itself comes from the Roman *imperator* which means an army commander who has won a great victory. On coins you will find the shortened forms of titles. For example, on a coin of the Emperor Claudius: TI CLAVD CAESAR AVG PM TRP IMP P P means *Tiberius Claudius Caesar Augustus Pontifex Maximus* (Chief Priest) *Tribune Imperator Pater Patriae* (Father of his Country).

CLAUDIUS

HADRIAN

Claudius   10 BC–AD 54
Proclaimed Emperor AD 41
Claudius was born in Lugdunum (now Lyons) in Gaul and had the misfortune to be the uncle of the mad and cruel Emperor Caligula. Caligula often had him thrown into the River Tiber at night just for fun. Claudius was a survivor, though, and when Caligula was murdered the soldiers proclaimed him emperor. He was a learned man noted for his great histories of the Etruscan and Carthaginian peoples. He is probably most famous for his invasion of Britain in AD 43 but he increased the Roman Empire by adding the provinces of Mauretania and Thracia as well. He was succeeded as emperor by Nero whom many suspected of killing both Claudius and Claudius' son, Britannicus.

Hadrian   AD 76–138
Proclaimed Emperor AD 117
Hadrian was born in Italica (now Seville) in Spain and as a child spent much of his time in the household of the Emperor Trajan who was born in the same city. He served in many parts of the Roman Empire both in the army and as a governor of various provinces. He travelled widely, because he was interested in the provinces and their peoples and also to make sure that the borders were well defended. He built two great lines of defence—Hadrian's Wall in Britain and the Limes in Germany (see page 41).

Constantine I   AD 272–337
Proclaimed Emperor AD 306
Constantinus was born at Naissus in Moesia and was proclaimed emperor by his troops in York on the death of his father. He claimed the western provinces but had to defeat other contestants for the throne. By AD 324 Constantine had defeated all his enemies. He moved the capital of the Roman Empire to Byzantium in AD 330 and renamed it after himself—Constantinople, the city of Constantine or 'New Rome'. He was known throughout his united empire as Constantine the Great. He was sympathetic to the Christian religion and was baptized into the faith shortly before his death.

CONSTANTINE I

City Centre

"In the forum both public and private business is controlled by the town's officials. The site of the basilica should be fixed next to the forum in as warm an area as possible so that in winter businessmen may meet there without being troubled by the weather."

Vitruvius, writing in the time of Augustus.

Vitruvius' guide for architects and builders describes all sorts of buildings for government, ceremony and religion which you would expect to find in the centre of any Roman town. These public buildings were usually grouped around the *forum*—an open area where business deals were made, or market stalls set up. It was also a place where people met for a chat—like a town square today. You will see a good example of a typical forum on page 47.

Sometimes the *forum* became so important for ceremonies and religion that is was no longer used as an open market place. Stall holders were often given a smaller *forum* or perhaps an enclosed market called a *macellum*. On the right is a reconstruction drawing of part of the most famous *forum* in the Roman world—the Roman Forum in Rome itself.

Processions and Temples for the Gods

In the scene on the right you are standing in the centre of the Roman Forum watching a religious procession. There are all sorts of statues here—of gods, goddesses and famous Romans. The procession has come past the Temple of Julius Caesar (in the centre of the picture). This magnificent building was constructed over the spot where Julius Caesar was cremated. To the right of the temple is the Triumphal Arch of the Emperor Augustus. Arches like this were usually built to celebrate victories. Victory is shown in her chariot on top of the arch.

Public Halls

In the Roman Forum there were also buildings which the Romans called *basilicas*. The large building in the foreground on the left is the *Basilica Aemilia*, named after Marcus Aemilius Lepidus who was *censor* in 179 BC. A *basilica* was a very large hall with an aisle on each side. It was used as an indoor meeting place—for law courts, social gatherings and for business.

S.BIESTY

The Army on the March

"The light-armed auxiliary troops and archers led the march to repel sudden enemy attacks. Next marched a troop of heavily-armed Roman soldiers, infantry and cavalry. They were followed by ten men from each centuria carrying their own kit and the equipment for marking out the camp. After them came the roadmakers to straighten the road."

The group of soldiers and engineers the historian, Josephus, describes led the army. Behind them came the commander's baggage, senior officers with cavalry to protect them and then the commander himself with the very best trained infantry and cavalry units. After the commander came cavalry, battering rams and artillery 'guns', officers, the standards of each unit and the trumpeters. The main body of the army marched six abreast with baggage and supplies following them. Mercenary soldiers and a strong force of infantry and cavalry protected the rear of this huge column.

If there was a new area to conquer, or a rebellion to put down in a province, or a campaign against 'barbarians' attacking the Empire's frontiers, then the Roman army came swiftly into action. By the time the Romans came to invade Britain in the mid 1st century AD there were 28 legions in the army. By this time each legion had about 5500 men in it and was divided into *cohorts* and subdivided into *centuriae*—centuries. Centurions still commanded these centuries. The rank above them, the *tribunes,* usually served in the army for a short time as part of their career in public life. Only a few stayed on as professional soldiers.

The legionary commander, called a *legatus,* was usually a senator appointed by the emperor. Only men who could be trusted commanded such large numbers of soldiers. One professional soldier helped the commander, and took over if he was away—called the camp *praefectus* or prefect.

Even in the Empire you still had to be a citizen to enlist in the army. Men who were not citizens could join the auxiliary forces, with the opportunity of being granted Roman citizenship on their discharge. These auxiliaries came from all over the

THE EMPIRE

Empire and often provided the Roman army with squadrons of experienced horsemen—the cavalry.

Discipline in the Roman army was hard, and often harsh. The centurions were responsible for training and for maintaining discipline. Discipline was necessary because the army had to put up with hard conditions in their camps and on the march. In battle the Roman army's superior training and obedience to orders often gave them the advantage over an enemy.

Scenes from Trajan's Column
Left: A photograph of a column put up in Rome by the emperor Trajan in AD *114. It stands as a memorial to his victory over the Dacians. Its detailed carving gives us a good idea of the Roman army in action. Details (top right) show a camp being built by the legionary soldiers. They are constructing a* rampart *or defensive wall from turfs carried in wickerwork baskets.*
Below left: the army is moving from the camp's gate onto a pontoon bridge. The standards here are those of each centuria.
Below right: attacking an enemy camp the legionaries are protected by locking their shields together. They called this a testudo—*the word means tortoise shell.*

The Army in Camp

"The infantry have armour to protect the chest, a helmet, and carry a blade on each side—a sword and a dagger. The infantry picked to form the general's bodyguard carry a spear and a round shield but other soldiers carry an oblong shield. Soldiers also carry a saw, basket, pick, axe, strap, bill-hook, chain and three-days' rations."

Every ordinary soldier was expected to carry as much as 30 kilograms while he was marching. Under the armour Josephus lists above the soldier wore a thick woollen tunic, sandals and a woollen cloak.

"The Romans never leave themselves open to a surprise attack of the enemy. In enemy territory they never engage in battle until they have built the defences of their camp."

This quotation from Josephus shows that the Roman army paid a great deal of attention to tactics employed against an enemy. Protecting the troops and equipment behind a strong fortification gave the Roman army an advantage against a less organized enemy.

Building the Camp

As in all armies there were rules and regulations for everything that was done. For each night an army spent outside its permanent fort, on manoeuvres or during a war, it built a fort. When the fort was constructed, so Josephus tells us, the ground was levelled if it was necessary and a rectangle marked out. The camp was measured out by the engineers who went ahead of the army on the march. In some cases the levelling was carried out by them as well. The main body of the troops dug the protective ditch and with the turf and soil from it made a great rampart.

Inside the camp's defences the tents for the officers would be put up in the centre, with those of the ordinary soldiers arranged in straight lines around. This allowed wide gaps, like streets, between the rows so that the men could assemble and rush to the defence of any part of their camp. The tents, as in the reconstruction drawing on the left, were made of pieces of leather sewn together. They were similar to ridge tents still used today.

Apart from the camp's fortifications of earth, everything was carried off for the next camp by the soldiers and their load-carrying animals. A Roman soldier might be expected to march as much as 30 kilometres (in about five hours) before making camp again.

Permanent Forts

Sometimes it was necessary for the Romans to build more permanent camps for their army units. These are usually known as forts—or fortresses if they were built for an entire legion. Roman forts were not all the same size or shape but they were regularly set out and you will often find the same types of building in the same place in every fort's design.

THE EMPIRE

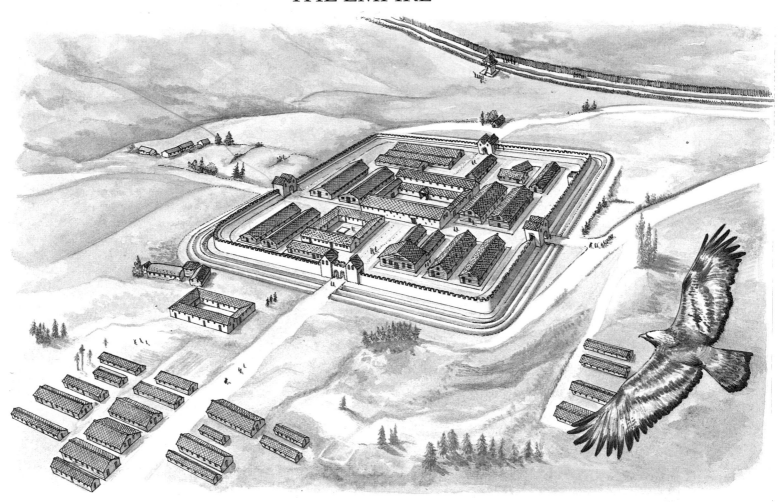

Josephus tells us something about the inside of a Roman fort: "The inside is measured out and streets laid down. In the centre are the officers' quarters, and the commander's HQ which looks like a temple. It seems like a town suddenly sprung up." The shape of the whole fort was usually rectangular with rounded corners (like the shape of a playing card), or square. The reconstruction drawing above is of the fort known as the Saalburg, near Frankfurt in Germany. It was built as one of the permanent forts of a northern defence line, called the *Limes*, from the River Rhine to the River Danube. You can see this defence beyond the fort—bank, ditch and wooden palisade or fence with its guard towers.

A reconstructed barrack building at the Saalburg. It is L-shaped with a large room for the centurion at one end. The other 10 rooms were for the 80 legionary soldiers, their weapons, baggage and equipment. The soldiers ate their meals in the barracks because there was no mess or communal dining room.

The fort's wall was built of stone with strongly constructed gates and guard towers. In the centre was the HQ. Elsewhere were storehouses, cookhouses, workshops and lavatories, and of course the barracks. Many buildings were needed for the unit of 500 men who lived here. Outside the fort's main gate a small village developed.

The Siege of Masada

There were many peoples in the Empire and neighbouring countries who objected to being ruled by the Romans. One example was a Celtic tribe called the Iceni in the province of Britain who were led in revolt against Roman rule by their queen Boudica. She lost against the superior military might of Rome, as did the Jews who lived in Syria and Palestine.

Jews Against the Romans

The Jews' struggle and eventual defeat in the area around Jerusalem, and in particular the siege of Masada in AD 74, was described by an eye-witness—an historian we have met before, Josephus. He himself was a Jew, and his name had originally been Joseph ben Matthias.

After Judaea had been taken over and ruled by governors the Romans found it difficult to control the various peoples who lived there. The Jews, Greeks and Samaritans were always fighting each other. In AD 66 violence erupted against the Romans and the garrison in Jerusalem was driven out.

An army of around 50,000 was sent, under the command of Vespasian and eventually his son Titus recaptured Jerusalem in AD 70. There were more than a million casualties there and Jewish prisoners were slaughtered in hundreds in amphitheatres in Syria and in Rome. Although Titus and Vespasian celebrated in AD 71 by building a magnificent triumphal arch in Rome, the campaign was not actually over. A group called the Sicarii had taken over the fortress at Masada in AD 73 and continued to defy the Romans. These Sicarii—the name the Romans gave them means bandit or murderer—were *zealots* who actively used violence to try to drive the Romans from their land. The Romans saw them as terrorists; they saw themselves as freedom fighters.

Romans Besiege Masada

We have a vivid account of the siege and attack of Masada by Josephus:

"The new governor in Judaea was Flavius Silva who saw that only one fortress held out against the Romans. The fortress was Masada. He built a siege wall right round the fortress, with camps, so that none of those besieged could easily escape."

Josephus then describes Flavius Silva's plan to break into the fortress. Look at the photo on the right. You will see a great ramp in the foreground and some of the camps for the Roman army. The ramp had once been a spur of rock ...

"The Romans occupied this and built a solid earth platform on top. On top of this they constructed a pier of stones. On this they built a tower 90 feet high protected all over with plates of iron. This tower was for the ballistas and stone-throwers. Silva also ordered a great battering ram to be swung continuously against the wall until it was beaten in one place."

The fortress, rebuilt by King Herod, had been constructed to stand a long siege. It had water cisterns, many storerooms and well-protected palaces. However, the Sicarii knew that there were not enough supplies to hold out against an entire legion. They hurriedly built a wooden wall inside Herod's stone one which had been broken down by the Roman battering ram. This last line of defence was burnt by the Roman attackers.

Death—The Jews' last protest against the Romans

Josephus now records a speech to the besieged Jews by their leader Eleazar Ben Ya'ir:

"It is clear that at daybreak our resistance will come to an end. But we are free to choose an honourable way to die with those we love. Let us die without becoming slaves to our enemies."

Josephus then records the final action of the besieged of Masada on April 15, AD 73:

"Ten were chosen by lot to be the rest's executioners and every one—men with their wives and children—lay down and offered their throats to those who had to perform the painful duty. So finally the nine presented their throats and the one man left until last set fire to the palace and drove his sword through his own body and fell down beside his family."

They preferred mass suicide rather than submit to the might of Rome. Josephus is able to record how many died that day—960 in all—because one woman with five children had hidden in a water cistern and was discovered by the Romans. Most of this account was checked when Masada was excavated by Israeli archaeologists in 1963–1965.

THE EMPIRE

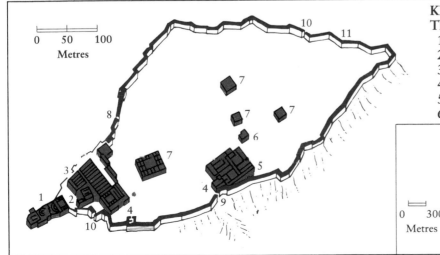

KEY A

The fortress of King Herod

1 King Herod's private palace
2 Baths
3 Storerooms
4 Offices
5 King Herod's official palace
6 Swimming pool
7 Apartment buildings
8 Snake Path Gate
9 West Gate
10 Water Gate
11 Underground water **reservoir**

KEY B

The Roman siege of Masada

1 Masada
2 Roman headquarters
3 Roman siege wall
4 Roman camps
5 The ramp
6 Snake Path to Masada

Trade in the Roman Empire

"So many merchant ships arrive in Rome with cargoes from everywhere, at all times of the year, and after each harvest, that the city seems like the world's warehouse. The arrival and departure of ships never stops—it's amazing that the sea, not to mention the harbour, is big enough for these merchant ships."

Aelius Aristides, 2nd century AD.

Even though the Empire was very large by the 2nd century AD a network of trade routes was established. Along these routes cargoes were carried, by ships, camels and carts to all parts of the Empire. A wealthy family living in Britain or Germany could have all the luxuries on offer from as far away as China and India. Traders could make sure that goods were carried quickly, too. A Roman cargo ship could cover about 160 kilometres in one day and even a caravan of camels travelled about 34 km in a day, according to Roman writers.

Even though private traders actually carried on the business of import and export, some goods were controlled by state officials. The Roman state controlled the corn and metal trades—precious metals such as gold and silver and others such as copper, tin, lead and iron.

Corn for the Dole

The trade in corn was probably the most important of all. It was obviously needed to feed people, especially in parts of the Empire where only small quantities could be grown. More importantly there had to be a large regular supply for the poor who could only survive by state handouts. In 2 BC there were 200,000 ordinary people registered in Rome for this free dole. An emperor, or town officials, could expect trouble and even riots if there was no free bread to hand out.

As you can see from the map all sorts of goods were moved about the Empire. Listed here are only the most important goods traded over a long distance. Farm produce of all sorts was carried, either fresh or dried, from place to place. Because of the popularity of shows in the amphitheatre wild animals were collected from many places. For example, deer and bears from Britain, elephants from India, hippos and crocodiles from Egypt, bison from Sarmatia and lions from Arabia.

Amphorae *were large pottery vessels used to transport fish sauce, olive oil, dried fruit, wine and other similar goods.*

Ostia—the Port of Rome

Ostia lies on the mouth of the River Tiber, 25 km from Rome, and had a number of very large warehouses belonging to import/export firms. At Ostia's Chamber of Commerce there were 61 offices for firms associated with sea trade. Each firm advertised its trade or service with a mosaic floor—this one is for the ships' carpenters or repairers.

THE EMPIRE

The Emperor Claudius had a new harbour and a lighthouse built at Ostia and the Emperor Trajan built another harbour there.

Large cargo ships were unloaded by ferry boats like the one in the painting above. It is from the tomb of a ferry-boat operator called Arascanius. The mast was used to tow the boat not to hold a sail.

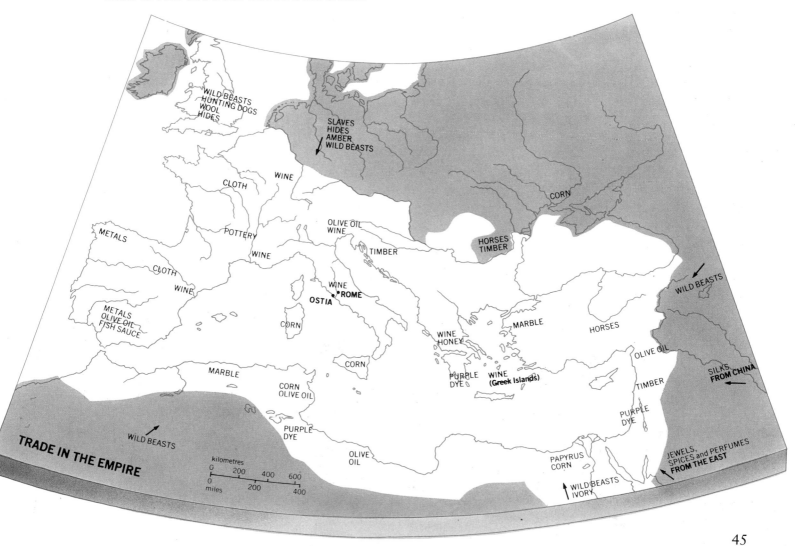

TRADE IN THE EMPIRE

A Roman Town: Pompeii

"On 24th August, at about 1 pm, my mother pointed out to uncle an odd-shaped cloud. We couldn't make out which mountain it came from but later found out that it was from Vesuvius. The cloud was rising in a shape rather like a pine tree because it shot up to a great height in the form of a tall trunk, then spread out at the top into branches."

The year was AD 79 and this is part of an account by an eye-witness of the eruption of Mount Vesuvius and the destruction of two important Roman cities, Pompeii and Herculaneum. The writer was Pliny, whom we have met before. He was staying with his uncle, the commander of the Roman fleet stationed at the nearby port of Misenum.

Pliny's uncle decided at first to investigate this extraordinary cloud which he said was "sometimes bright, sometimes dark as if full of earth and cinders". But then he received reports that people were in danger and decided to send in the fleet to help the survivors. Pliny tells us that his uncle died—suffocated by sulphur fumes—trying to get back to his ship.

We imagine volcanoes pouring out molten lava, but Vesuvius rained ash, pumice-stone and lava-stone pebbles down onto the nearby towns. Some, a long way away like Naples, were just covered with a thin layer of ash. Pompeii is only 8.5 km away from the volcano and ash and stones nearly 4 metres deep covered the town. Herculaneum was filled with a mudflow caused by the eruption. By the time the sky had cleared three days later all the towns in the Bay of Naples had suffered—some, like Pompeii and Herculaneum, could not be lived in again.

From a population of 20,000 about 2000 people died at Pompeii. Everyone in the cities and farms near the volcano lost their homes. The Roman poet Martial said that "everything is

Right: Both people and animals were suffocated by the volcanic fumes. Their bodies slowly rotted away inside the ash which fell and solidified into moulds around them. You can pour liquid plaster into the spaces which were left and recover almost perfect casts. This guard dog was chained up outside a house, perhaps forgotten by its owners or perhaps they too were suffocated. Favourite Roman names for dogs were Ferox *(Fierce) and* Celer *(Swift).*

Left: This illustration of an excavation is from a guide book to Pompeii of 1881. Notice the height of the surface of the ground above the buildings. Thousands of people visited Pompeii in the 19th century, and many more read about the latest discoveries. This scene shows the uncovering of a bakery with the millstones for grinding the flour on the right and the oven in the background, complete with bread, which was ready for customers in the afternoon of 24 August AD 79.

drowned in the flames and buried in the ashes of sadness". The emperor at the time, Titus, set up a special team of senators to hand out relief, mainly money, to the refugees of the Naples area. Titus even set up a fund to rebuild the cities but nothing was ever done—the cities were buried too deep.

The Roman Towns Rediscovered

Pompeii and Herculaneum were gradually forgotten and it was not until 1594 that their sites were rediscovered. Excavations to uncover the cities began in the 18th century but they were not at all like the careful archaeological work you have read about earlier in this book. These excavations were like hunting parties on the lookout for beautiful objects, like statues. The searchings of these treasure hunters did an enormous amount of damage to both Pompeii and Herculaneum.

In 1860 a new director of excavations of Pompeii was appointed – Giuseppe Fiorelli. Unlike many of the previous excavators who had burrowed down inside individual buildings he worked very carefully uncovering whole streets. He also invented the technique of taking plaster casts, like the one of the dog on the left.

It wasn't just buildings which Fiorelli and later

This photograph taken from the air shows the town of Pompeii. Excavations in the 18th and 19th centuries uncovered very large areas which had to be protected or conserved. You can actually go inside some of the buildings today because they have been partly rebuilt with their roofs on. The open area on the left is the forum, in the centre are the two theatres and on the far right an amphitheatre. Look for all these buildings in the plan on the next page.

archaeologists uncovered in Pompeii. Most of the objects which people used every day were left behind in the mad rush to escape the fury of the volcano. Unlike the objects found on most archaeological excavations those at Pompeii and Herculaneum are usually found in good condition. Some objects not normally found at all on excavations—for example, bread—have been found because they were burnt and turned into *carbon*. Look back to page 46 and you will see the excavators removing perfectly preserved loaves of bread from an oven.

A ROMAN TOWN: POMPEII

Graffiti—Scribblings on Walls

Another interesting type of *evidence* about the people uncovered during the excavations, and not often found elsewhere, is the *graffiti* or scribblings. The people of Pompeii loved scribbling on walls. Some of it was useful information. For example, lists of market days at nearby towns (Saturday in Pompeii) or adverts for games in the amphitheatre:

> "The gladiators owned by Aulus Suettius Certus will fight at Pompeii on May 31st. There will be an animal hunt and awnings will be provided."

or just scribbled messages like:

> "Successus the cloth-weaver loves Iris, the innkeeper's slave-girl."

or

> "A bronze pot has disappeared from the shop ... a reward for anyone who returns it."

Near the Temple of Venus various stalls were set up to provide worshippers with offerings for the goddess. One stallholder wrote: "Verecunnus cake-seller here". Someone, perhaps tired at seeing so many walls covered in graffiti wrote:

> "I am surprised, O Wall, that you have not fallen down in ruins with the weight of all this scribbled rubbish."

Pompeii—the Town Plan

There was a town at Pompeii long before the Romans took over this part of Italy. It was founded by the Osci but was enlarged as a trading town by the Greeks in the 6th century BC. The Greeks built a wall to enclose the area they wanted the town to extend into and to keep out the Etruscans. For a short time the Samnites occupied and developed Pompeii but in 290 BC, during the wars with the Samnites, they were thrown out by the Romans.

The town continued to flourish and in 80 BC it was declared a *colonia*—that is, a town for retired soldiers and their families to settle in. There was a lot of new building and rebuilding at this time. For example, the small theatre (called an *odeon*) and the amphitheatre (built for 20,000 spectators) were both built in 80 BC. During the 1st century AD it became a rich trading town famous for its millstones (there was plenty of local lava-stone), a sauce made from fish, perfumes and cloth.

> "When the walls of the town are built the next thing to do is to lay out the main streets and alleyways."
> *Vitruvius, architect at the time of Augustus.*

Both the Greeks and the Romans tried to set out their towns in an orderly way. You can see that the area (about 65 hectares) enclosed by the Greek wall on the plan below is divided into a number of regular areas for houses. The Romans called these *insulae* (the word means islands); we would call them blocks.

The Town Centre

The oldest part of the town is around the *forum*. We have already seen how important this part of the town was. Around the open *forum* with its pavement protected by a roof held up by columns were a variety of buildings. Some were religious—temples to the gods Jupiter, Apollo, the Emperor Vespasian and Lares (the town's own gods).

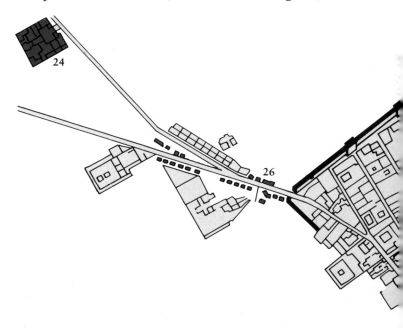

Other buildings were for the government of the town—the hall for voting (*comitium*), the offices of the chief councillors and the council chamber and the *basilica* (a great public hall). Finally there were buildings for trade and business—a little market hall, the market for clothmakers, another for the corn trade. There were also the weights and measures offices set up by the town council to make sure that goods were being sold according to regulations.

A ROMAN TOWN: POMPEII

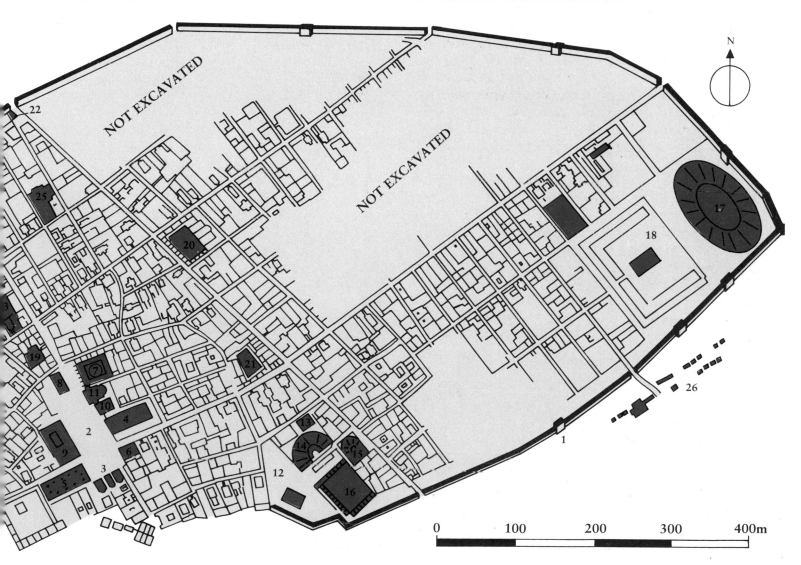

Public Services

When a town council decided to develop a new part of town they had to think about services for the townspeople. The most important was a good water supply. Second was a proper system of drains. Both of these were linked with the laying out of streets, and in some cases, as at Pompeii, pavements.

Water Supply

The Romans took the problem of water supply very seriously as they needed such large amounts for drinking, baths and lavatories. Various devices were used to create this water supply. Even if the land was suitable to sink wells for water much more was needed in a town—and it had to be running water. The most common way of supplying this was to build an *aqueduct*—the word simply means a way of 'bringing water'.

An aqueduct was usually just a water channel cut across country from a good source (such as a river or a spring) to the town or city. It might be just a channel cut into the ground (like a ditch) or lined with stone like a proper drain. Sometimes it had to go underground and arched tunnels were needed. Sometimes the Roman engineers were faced with more difficult problems. Aqueducts sometimes had to bridge rivers or valleys like the Pont-du-Gard aqueduct on page 6. The aqueduct bringing water to Pompeii started 40 km away to the east.

The water was brought to a reservoir, called a *castellum aquae,* in the town. In Pompeii it was near the gate facing Vesuvius. This reservoir supplied a number of lead tanks on towers about 6 metres high throughout the town. Fourteen tanks have been found in the excavations so far. Lead pipes carried the water to houses, shops, baths and public fountains in the streets.

The town appointed an official to look after the supply of water—called a *curator aquarum.* He had a team of workmen and engineers to maintain the supply. This meant cleaning the system, repairing it and trying to stop people from tapping off their own private supply! Some of the problems of the water inspector were recorded by Frontinus in his 'book' called *The Water Supply of Rome* which he wrote when he was the *curator aquarum* in AD 97:

"The inspector must make sure that no one draws more water from the public system than he has permission for from the Emperor. He must be on his guard all the time against the many forms of fraud."

Although not everyone had a water supply in their house or flat, there were plenty of public fountains in the streets of Pompeii.
Right: A stone-built water tank with a permanent jet of water supplied by lead pipes under the pavement.
Below: Water spouts on the tanks were often carved like this one—it's a water god.

A ROMAN TOWN: POMPEII

The Surveyor

The architect, the surveyor and the builder were responsible for putting up a town's buildings. To set out either a whole town or an individual building, careful and accurate measurements were essential. The surveyor had a number of instruments to help him. On the left is a drawing of a *groma*. Once it was set into the ground and the plumb-lines showed that it was upright the surveyor could sight out straight lines and right angles.

A more complex instrument to sight level lines was the *dioptra*—like the level or theodolite surveyors use today. There was also an instrument called a *chorobates*, like a spirit level, to see if surfaces in buildings were level.

Despite the difficulties Frontinus estimated that he could provide 1000 million litres of water each day for the people of Rome.

Streets

Unlike many towns Pompeii had a stone surface to its streets and the edge of the pavements. There was plenty of stone in the area for this work. Notice in the photograph on the left how the surface of the street has been worn into ruts—by the iron bands on cart wheels. See also that the water tank has large stones at the corners which jut out onto the street to protect it from traffic. Can you see the very large blocks of stone crossing the street? They are stepping stones. Pompeii had no proper system of drains—everything flowed along the canal-like streets.

Right: A crane in use on the repair of a public arch in Pompeii—the Arch of the Emperor Caligula. The crane is made of wood and is 'powered' by men working a treadmill.

Sport and Leisure

At the Baths

"I live over the public baths—you know what that means. Ugh! It's sickening. First there are the 'strongmen' doing their exercises and swinging heavy lead weights about with grunts and groans. Next there are the lazy ones having a cheap massage—I can hear someone being slapped on the shoulders. Then there is the noise of a brawler or a thief being arrested and the man who always likes the sound of his own voice in the bath. And what about the ones who leap into the pool making a huge splash as they hit the water!"

Lucius Seneca, around AD *63.*

Unless they actually lived over a bath-house, not many people would have agreed with Lucius Seneca. A bath-house was considered essential in any Roman town and most towns had more than one. Everyone went to the baths—it was cheap enough for both rich and poor to go frequently and children got in free. But it is a mistake to think that the Romans went to the baths simply to get clean. That was only one part of an enjoyable way to spend several hours. Some people seemed to spend a long time at the baths—someone in the baths at Pompeii had scribbled on the wall, "Jarinus you live here". The baths were somewhere to meet friends for a chat, a game of dice or to sort out some business deal.

Cold, Hot and Steamy Rooms

What, then were the baths like? This is what Lucian wrote in one of his *Satires* on life in the Roman world in the 2nd century AD:

"When you enter the baths you are received into a large hall with plenty of rooms for servants and bath attendants ... next are the locker rooms to undress in ... you come into

S BIESTY

another room slightly warmed instead of meeting you with a fierce blast of heat ... next is the hot room and in the room beyond three hot tubs. When you have bathed, you need not go back through these rooms—you can go straight into the cold room."

Look at the reconstruction drawing below and see which rooms Lucian is talking about. This is one of the three public baths at Pompeii—the smallest, next to the forum. Beyond the drawing was the locker room, called the *apodyterium.* Next to that was the *tepidarium,* the warm room. It's in the drawing—the men are sitting on benches with their towels in niches around the walls. In front of that (far left in the drawing) is the hot room, the *caldarium.* This room would not only be hot but also steamy like a modern Turkish bath. In the *caldarium* there were sometimes baths of hot water sunk into the floor as well as steaming tubs. There might also be a *laconicum* nearby—a very hot, but dry, room like a sauna. But where did all the heat come from for these hot rooms? Part of the answer is on the far left of the drawing. You will see that the floor of the hot room is raised on little pillars. A furnace drove hot air under the floor and through air-channels in the walls and vaulted roofs. The Romans called this system the *hypocaust.*

In the centre of the drawing (look through the columns) you can see the cold room—the *frigidarium.* It has a dip bath in it to freshen you up after exercise in the courtyard, the *palaestra,* which you can see on the far right.

Men and women did not bath together and baths usually had separate sessions for each. This one at Pompeii had a completely separate women's baths with its own hot and cold rooms. Furnaces built together served both sets of baths. A large staff of slaves would be needed for all sorts of jobs—keeping the baths clean and the fires going, serving snacks and drinks, massaging or even plucking hair from the armpits of customers. An essential job was to scrape the customers clean after a hot steamy bath or exercise. They rubbed oil over the skin and scraped off the dirt with a curved instrument called a *strigilis.*

Gladiators

Some of the most important public buildings in any Roman town were those built for entertainment. People all over the Roman world went in very large crowds to see the gladiators in the amphitheatre, Greek and Roman plays in the theatre, concerts and poetry readings in little theatres and halls and chariot racing in the stadium.

Cruelty and Death—Called Entertainment
During 'shows' the amphitheatre was often filled with the screams of dying people, the frightened cries of animals and the shouts and cheers of the crowds. In the Colosseum in Rome 50,000 people regularly thronged to the various sorts of bloody entertainment on offer. Pompeii's amphitheatre held 20,000 spectators.

The Fighters
First, there were fights between *gladiators*. These men were highly trained and usually fought to the death. The pairs of fighters were well matched for an exciting contest. Some were heavily armed with a sword and shield and body armour, others may have carried a net and a three-pronged spear. The types of weapon and armour carried by the gladiators gave them different names: a Gaul carried a sword and a shield; a Samnite was heavily armed with a shield and axe and his body was completely covered with armour; a Thracian had a round shield and a curved dagger.

Gladiators were usually slaves who had been captured in war. Their chances of survival were small, but a few were given their freedom if they fought well and gave 'good value for money'.

Animal Fights
Animal fights and large scale hunts were also staged in the amphitheatre. There were specially constructed cages under the floor (called an *arena*—which means sand, used to soak up the blood) in many amphitheatres. Now that the floor is missing in the Colosseum (right) you can see where the cages were. The cages allowed wild animals to be raised to the surface of the arena without too much danger to their keepers. It also made possible a dramatic entry for ferocious or exotic animals. All sorts of animal were gathered for these shows—panthers, lions, hyaenas, bears, rhinos, elephants, zebras, giraffes, wild boars, deer, wild horses and snakes. How many of these animals can you see in the mosaic floor (below) from a house in Lepcis Magna in North Africa?

Left: This decorated pot was made in Colchester in the province of Britain in about AD 200. The whole pot shows an animal hunt, bear-baiting and a contest between two gladiators. You can see a heavily-armed man fighting a net-man, called a retiarius. *An inscription around the top gives their names—MEMNON and VALENTINUS (on the right). Notice that Valentinus is holding up one finger. It shows that he has been beaten by Memnon—see his three-pronged spear on the ground—and is asking the crowds for mercy.*

SPORT AND LEISURE

Flooding the amphitheatre for sea battles also allowed crocodiles, hippos and seals to form part of the entertainment. Sometimes the animals were trained to perform tricks for the crowds as well. Normally, though, they were hunted and slaughtered—sometimes killing a few of the hunters along the way.

Reactions to the Games

Not all Romans approved of killing.

"I happened to call in at a midday show in the amphitheatre, expecting some sport, fun and relaxation. It was just the opposite. By comparison the fights that had already taken place were merciful. Now they really get down to business—it's sheer murder. In the morning men are thrown to the lions or bears—at noon they are thrown to the spectators."

Seneca.

"The wild animal hunts, two every day for five days, are magnificent—I wouldn't deny it. But what pleasure can it give a person of taste when either a feeble human being is torn to pieces by an incredibly strong wild animal or a handsome beast is transfixed by a spear?"

Cicero.

Watching so much violence and death in the arena often led to fighting among the crowds, as happened in Pompeii in AD 59:

"There was a serious riot between the people of Pompeii and Nuceria, a nearby town. It all started with a small incident at a gladiatorial show. Insults were hurled, then stones and finally swords were drawn. The locals from Pompeii came out of it best—a number of Nucerians were taken off wounded or dead."

Tacitus.

Colosseum

"What nation is so remote, Emperor, or so barbarous that someone hasn't come from it to watch the games in your city? There are farmers from the Balkans here, natives from southern Russia bred on horse's blood, people who drink the Nile's waters and even those from far away Britain. Arabs, people from the shores of the Red Sea, as well as those from southern Turkey, have hurried here and German tribesmen and Ethiopians each with their own peculiar hairstyles."

This poem by Martial was addressed to the Emperor Titus in AD 80 to celebrate the opening of the Amphitheatrum Flavium (above). Later it got the name of Colosseum from a colossal statue of the Emperor Nero which stood nearby.

Chariot Racing

"The races do not interest me at all. If you've seen one race you've seen them all. I cannot understand why so many thousands of people want to see horses racing and men driving chariots—why don't they grow up?"

Well you can see what the writer Pliny thought about the popular sport of chariot racing. His view was certainly not shared by many people living all over the Roman world who flocked to the race-tracks in or near their towns and cities. What was a 'day at the races' in Rome like?

It begins with a rather serious ceremony called a *pompa* in which officials, priests and priestesses leading statues of gods and goddesses, musicians and dancers and the charioteers parade through Rome to the *stadium*—the Circus Maximus. The huge crowd is already seated—or rather leaping about, waving and shouting excitedly.

The spectators have already placed bets on which team will win in the first race. There are four teams—the Reds, the Blues, the Greens and the Whites. Pliny, again, has a word to say about the fanatical betting:

"I wouldn't mind if the spectators went to see the speed of the horses or the skill of the charioteers. But all they support is the colour of the driver's tunic. If they swapped colours in mid-race, I swear they'd follow the colours and change their support too."

The charioteers line up their chariots, usually drawn by four horses, in the *carceres,* the stalls. The official in charge of the games drops the white cloth, the *mappa,* as the signal to start—and they're off! The horses leap and gallop, the wheels of the lightweight chariots whir on the hard sand and the charioteers whip on the horses. The most dangerous time in the race is at the three turning points, the *metae,* at each end of the central barrier called the *spina.* Look for them in the carving on the right.

At the *metae* the chariots sometimes ride on one wheel as the charioteers try to gain those extra seconds which might help them to win. Quite often there is a crash—the Romans call it a 'shipwreck'. It must have looked like that; perhaps the chariot had broken up in the crash, the horses running across the track still yoked together, the charioteer desperately trying to cut himself free of the reins to avoid being trampled to death.

There were seven laps in all and the whole race was about 6·5 km. Each lap was indicated to the crowd by great wooden eggs, *ova,* on stands in the central barrier. The winner, finally, was the charioteer who crossed the white line marked out in front of the judges' stand. To the deafening cheer of the crowd he received a victor's crown and later a purse of gold. It was usual to have 24 races each day.

Charioteers—Rich and Famous

Some charioteers became famous and were treated like heroes. A few even had their own fan clubs. The followers of one charioteer called Sorbus carried his pictures with them to the races and waved them about. Successful charioteers could also become very rich. One, Diocles, became a millionaire and had his career recorded on a stone monument in Rome in AD 146. Part of it says:

"Gaius Appuleius Diocles, charioteer of the Red Stable, a Spaniard by birth, aged 42 years 7 months 23 days. He drove chariots for 24 years, ran 4257 starts and won 1462 victories. He made 9 horses 100-time winners, and one a 200-time winner. The Champion of all charioteers. He excelled the charioteers of all the stables who ever participated in the races of the circus games."

Below: The huge building (it's 600 metres long) began as a simple race track around a stream which ran across this valley in Rome. It was gradually added to and rebuilt so that 100,000 spectators could watch the races by the 1st century BC. It became larger and more elaborate under the emperors. Augustus had a special temple built for the gods who looked after the races (middle top in the drawing) and brought an obelisk, *a tall carved column, from Egypt to decorate the* spina. *After a time, in AD 64, the Emperor Nero rebuilt the Circus Maximus so that it could hold 250,000 fans. However, the arrangements for them were not always safe. In the 3rd century AD about 13,000 people were killed when temporary wooden seating collapsed. Despite this, by the 4th century AD it had been enlarged again to hold 350,000.*

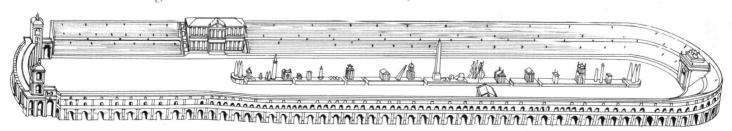

At the Theatre

The Romans looked back to the Greeks as far as the theatre was concerned—both for the types of play they enjoyed and for the building they used for performances. At first Roman theatres put on just Greek tragedies (serious plays) and comedies. Then Roman plays began to be written. There were four types of play you could see in a Roman theatre.

Fabula Palliata was copied from Greek plays and the actors wore Greek dress. *Fabula Atellana* was a slapstick farce about country life and included characters all theatregoers would recognize—*Maccus* the clown, *Bucco* the clown with puffed-out cheeks, *Pappus* the silly old man and *Dossenus* the clever hunchback. *Fabula Praetexta* was a tragedy based on history, legends or current events. *Fabula Togata* was a comedy based on village life.

It wasn't only full-length plays which were put on in the theatre. Romans also enjoyed two other types of stage production. The *mimus*, from which the word mime comes, was a sketch or short scene about city life. Unlike the full-length plays, women were allowed to act in them. As the name suggests there was a lot of mimicry or imitation of people, animals and birds. These sketches also contained singing and dancing and were usually about the sorts of goings-on your parents would not like you to see on the stage!

Then there was the *pantomimus* which was not at all what you might think. It was a sort of ballet with music. There was only one actor who changed costume and mask for each character and mimed the action of the story while singers and a chorus sang out in the background. Favourite stories for the *pantomimus* were tales and legends from the past.

The Theatre Building

What were the theatre buildings like? Their D shape was copied from the Greeks. Look at examples of Roman theatres in this book: one in Cyprus on page 7, one at Pompeii on page 47 and a theatre interior on pages 60 and 61. The audience sat on a steep slope around, and often also in, the semi-circular area. In Greek plays the chorus danced and sang here. It was sometimes used in Roman plays but more often was full of the rich and important who brought fold-away

Actors wore special masks and costumes to help the audience recognize the sorts of character they were playing. Coloured wigs indicated the type of person—red for slaves, black for young men, white for old men. Costume, too, was fixed—old men wore white, young men wore purple and women yellow. In this mosaic from a house in Pompeii you can see actors preparing for a Greek play. On the left two are practising dance steps while a musician plays the double pipes. In front of the man who is sitting (perhaps this is the author) there are two masks. Behind him is another mask and an actor being helped into his costume.

seats to be near the stage—front row privileges!

The stage itself was very elaborate so that, although they had stage 'sets', the stone built background could be used in plays where a grand house or a public building was called for. Vitruvius, the architect, says this of stage design:

"On either side of the stage are the spaces for scenery. These are called *periaktoi* in Greek from three-sided machines which revolve giving a different scene on each side. These turn and present a different view to the audience when there are changes in the play or when the gods appear with sudden claps of thunder."

SPORT AND LEISURE

The stage had all sorts of other devices that the audience must have enjoyed—for example, trap doors, lots of entrances and exits, and hoists for lifting actors off the stage. The theatre on the next page is the main one at Pompeii built to take an audience of more than 5000. It is shown open to the sky but it also had an awning, called a *velarium,* which protected the audience from the sun and rain.

You will see a smaller indoor theatre marked on the plan of Pompeii on page 49. This type of theatre was called an *odeon.* It was used for concerts, lectures, poetry readings and musical competitions. Although these concert halls were usually smaller than theatres, the one built at Lugdunum (now Lyons) in Gaul was enlarged to hold about 10,500 people—concerts were popular there!

The Emperor Nero loved performances in the odeon—but usually only when he was performing himself! Actually he had a go at chariot racing and acting as well as recitals. One writer, Suetonius, comments rather sourly about the Emperor's musical talents:

> "It was forbidden to leave the theatre during a recital by Nero—however urgent the reason—and the gates were kept locked. We read of women in the audience giving birth and of men who were so bored with the music that they pretended to be dead and were carried away to be buried!"

Off to See a Play

So, what was seeing a play in a Roman theatre like? You could sit where you wanted (except right at the front) for nothing. If the theatre had a curtain it was lowered into a slot at the front of the stage to reveal the first scene of the play. It was very noisy with the audience shouting out encouragement or insults to the actors. Actors, too, sometimes shouted back at the audience! Everyone seemed to enjoy themselves, though, and people in Rome could see stage performances on 100 days *each year* by the mid 4th century AD.

The play being acted in our reconstruction drawing on the next pages is by Plautus who wrote during the 2nd century BC. The play, a comedy called *The Rope,* has a simple story with the sorts of character loved by Roman audiences. A young man called Plesidippus has fallen in love with a slave girl, Palaestra and, of course, they cannot get married. There is a happy ending, though, when Palaestra turns out to be free-born after all. The secret is contained in a trunk washed ashore and recovered by a slave fisherman, Gripus. He is seen carrying the trunk with a rope trailing from it. The rope is grabbed by Trachalio, the slave of Plesidippus, who is determined to get hold of the trunk.

Now turn the page and read on . . .

Masks, like costume, helped the audience sort out the characters. This one is for the hero in a Greek tragedy. Masks were also useful for the actors as they could use them as sound boxes to project their voices in the vast theatres.

"*Trachalio:* Hey you, hold on!
Gripus: What for?
Trachalio: Wait while I wind up this rope for you.
Gripus: Oi, leave it alone.
Trachalio: Oh, I'm only trying to be helpful—one good turn deserves another you know.
Gripus: It's no good asking me for fish, young man—the sea was too rough last night. I didn't catch any. Look—a net dripping with water but no fish.
Trachalio: Honestly, I'm not looking for fish. I'm more interested in a little chat.
Gripus: I don't care who you are—just stop bothering me.
Trachalio: Hey, hang on. Not so fast.
Gripus: What?
Trachalio: That trunk. I've known its owner for a long time.
Gripus: What do you mean?
Trachalio: And I know how it got lost.
Gripus: Do you now? Well I know how it was found and I know who found it and I know who owns it now. Nobody is going to get it away from me and don't you try it.
Trachalio: Wait a minute, you. Did you ever see a fisherman catch a fish like a trunk or offer one for sale? Make up your mind whether you're a fisherman or a trunk-maker. Go on, tell me, how can a trunk be a fish? I won't let you carry off anything that hasn't got scales on it.
Gripus: What? You've never heard of a trunk-fish?
Trachalio: Rubbish, there's no such fish.
Gripus: Oh yes there is—I'm a fisherman, I know. Of course, they are very rarely caught—they don't often come near land.
Trachalio: Don't think you can fool me. What colour are these trunk-fish?
Gripus: They come in all sorts of colours. A few this colour but I've seen them purple and the big ones are black.
Trachalio: I bet they are. Well, you'll find yourself turning into a trunk-fish if you're not very careful. First you'll turn purple and then black and blue!"

We find out that the trunk belongs to Palaestra. She turns out to be the long-lost daughter of Daemones who happens to be living on the coast near to where the shipwreck was. The story ends happily ever after—father and daughter are re-united; she marries Plesidippus.

60

Public and Community Life

Religion

The Romans originally believed that powerful spirits, which they called *numina*, controlled everything. These spirits could be encouraged to be friendly if the right offerings and prayers were made to them. As they came into contact with other peoples, the Romans adopted other religious ideas. They began to worship gods who looked like humans, had names and particular duties. Most important to the Romans was *Jupiter* whom they called the 'greatest and best' of the gods. Others were:

Juno—Jupiter's wife who looked after women.
Mars—god of war, also worshipped by farmers.
Vulcan—god of fire, pictured with a thunderbolt.
Saturn—a god of wine, especially worshipped at the festival of the Saturnalia from 17th to 23rd of December. All shops, businesses, public offices and schools were closed.
Minerva—goddess of wisdom, crafts, industries and trade.
Venus—goddess of beauty and fertility.
Mercury—god of merchants who also carried the messages of the gods with his winged sandals and hat.
Vesta—goddess of the earth and sacred fire.
Janus—a two-headed god whom the Romans supposed created the world. His temple in the Forum in Rome remained open in times of war, closed when there was peace—the doors were rarely closed.

This temple, called the Pantheon—'to all the Gods'—was built in this form by the Emperor Hadrian between AD 118 and 125. The building has survived because it has been used as a Christian church since AD 609.

As their empire extended, other gods and goddesses were allowed to be worshipped in Rome itself. Isis, for example, an Egyptian goddess, was a favourite. It is not surprising, therefore, to learn that the Romans could be very adaptable in their views about the sorts of worship carried out in the provinces of the Empire. They were tolerant—but only up to a point. They were suspicious of any religious worship which seemed to threaten the Roman state itself and its authority over the peoples of the Empire. The Romans tried to eliminate, by laws, persecution and even war, the religions of both the Jews and the Christians. They would not tolerate the worship of the Druids in Gaul and Britain.

A Roman Celtic Goddess
A good example of how the Romans were able to adapt to the new religious ideas of the peoples they conquered was in the town of Bath in Britain,

Emperor Marcus Aurelius making sacrifices to the gods, 2nd century AD. Marcus Aurelius had been made a priest of the god Mars when he was only eight years old.

A bronze statue, only 44 mm high, of a stag. It was left as an offering in a temple outside the Roman town of Camulodunum (now Colchester) in Britain.

called by them *Aquae Sulis*. This literally means the Waters of the Sun-Goddess Sul. Sul was a Celtic goddess and a particular favourite of people in the Bath area. After the Roman conquest, a magnificent temple was built in honour of a new goddess called Sulis Minerva—a combination of the Celtic Sul and the Roman goddess Minerva.

Emperors were Gods too

Listed among the most important gods during the Empire were the emperors themselves. Sometimes they were worshipped as gods even before they died but usually then in temples outside Rome itself.

There were many other less important gods and goddesses worshipped by the Romans. Each house had a little altar set up for the special 'gods of the household'. In the family it was the head of the family who made offerings to the gods on the family's behalf.

The Romans did not worship their gods in the way some people worship their god today. They did not go to the temple to attend a service. The gods were worshipped at special festivals with processions like the one on pages 36 and 37. Offerings and prayers could be made to them at any time. The priest or priestess made offerings on

behalf of the people as did the *pontifex maximus*, chief priest, on behalf of the Roman state. We have already seen that the emperor was often the state's chief priest.

Sometimes sacrifices of animals were made to the gods but it was more often offerings of fruit, cheese and cakes made with honey. They usually made a *libation*, that is pouring out milk or wine as an offering.

Christianity

The Christian religion was practised in many parts of the Roman world, though often in secret because of persecution. Christians were not allowed to bury their dead in cemeteries in Rome and used the *catacombs* instead—an extraordinary series of underground tombs you can still visit today. It was here that illegal services were sometimes held. After centuries of persecution Christianity was accepted as the official Roman religion by decree of the Emperor Constantine I in AD 312. After that, of course, many Romans still worshipped the old gods.

The inscription reads:
"To the god Silvanus, the King of the Woods. Cintusmus the coppersmith willingly and gladly carries out his obligation."

The inscription, 80 mm across, was found during the excavation of the same temple from which the little stag came. Both objects are dated to the 2nd century AD. It was common for the followers of a particular god to place or nail up in a temple a record of a vow or obligation which had been carried out. We are not often told what the vow was. Perhaps the stag and the inscription go together and Cintusmus asked the King of the Woods for a good stag to kill when he went out hunting.

Ceremonies

Getting Married

"Dear Junius Mauricus, You ask me to look for a husband for your niece. Minicius Acilianus is the right man. He is a gentleman and his face is fresh looking. He's a handsome man, every inch a senator."

This is part of a letter from Pliny to a friend. It shows that marriages in the Roman world were usually arranged, just as they are still in some countries today.

The couple to be married were probably quite young when they became engaged. The girl was usually twelve and the boy fourteen when a special ceremony, called the *sponsalia,* took place. The future husband would give the girl gifts, usually a ring, a contract would be signed and the whole affair would be sealed with a kiss.

Next came the question of choosing the right day—the Romans were very superstitious. Certain festival days were thought unlucky, like the feast for the dead, the *Parentalia,* which took place between 18th and 21st of February. The Romans thought that the best and luckiest time to get married was during the second half of June.

The Ceremony

There were various forms of marriage ceremony but the most elaborate was called the *confarreatio.* The ceremony took place in the bride's home. The bride wore a pure white tunic and a flame-coloured veil over her head with sandals matching the colour of her veil. A sacrifice was made, usually of a pig, so that omens or signs could be looked for in its innards. The woman said the words, *"Ubi tu Gaius, ego Gaia"* which meant "Whichever family you belong to, I also belong". All the guests called out "Good luck!" and the marriage was then sealed.

The man led his wife to his own house where she was carried over the threshold to avoid stumbling which the Romans considered very unlucky.

Death and Burial

"I have journeyed through many countries and across many seas too ... I come to these sad offerings for you, my dead brother ... to speak to your silent ashes ... Oh, what is the use ... Hail and goodbye for ever, dear brother."

This is part of a poem by Catullus. The Romans, of course, felt grief for those who died but probably showed it more than people do in Western Europe and America today. The Romans not only cried but would also beat their chests and go about with torn clothes and their hair in a mess. Some people even paid for professional mourners to do this job for them.

The body would be placed on a bed with torches and candles burning at each corner. Quite often pine cones or small branches would be burnt

This marriage ceremony is sealed by the couple joining hands. Some of the guests on the right are holding the traditional sweets and sesame cakes. Nuts were thrown to the children for luck.

to give off a rich smell. Perhaps this was to hide the smell as the corpse was supposed to lie in the house for about a week. Poor people could expect a funeral the day after death.

If the person was important, or just rich, the corpse would be carried on a *bier* or litter to some public place in the town and a public speech, called a *laudatio,* was made about his or her life. The procession was rather grand as you can see from the drawing below. Trumpet players went in front of the bier which would be carried by slaves. Then there might be torch carriers, those professional mourners and actors representing the dead person's relatives and then the relatives themselves.

The body might then be cremated and the ashes put into a specially-made jar, or buried in the ground. Burial became more common than cremation in the 2nd century AD in the Roman world. By law bodies had to be buried outside the limits or walls of the town. Cemeteries were often alongside the roads. If you were poor you could expect no more than a simple plot in an overcrowded cemetery. If you had some money you might have had a tombstone like the one on page 66. If you were rich your family might have had a large vault or tomb called a *columbarium.* Slaves of the family would be buried here too.

The Romans believed that the dead went to live in the underworld with the gods of the dead—the *Manes.* Offerings were made to these gods by pouring out wine or leaving food at the graveside, first of all nine days after burial then at special festivals throughout the year.

Everyday Life

In the Family

"Pompeius Catussa, a plasterer, put up this memorial to his wife, Blandinia Martiola, who was without any fault and very kind to him. Whoever reads this, go and bathe in the Baths of Apollo, as I used to with my wife. I wish I still could."
From a tombstone found at Lugdunum (now Lyons), Gaul.

The Romans considered marriage and the family a very important part of their society. There are many scenes of happy parents and their children to be found among Roman writings and in carvings on stone.

However, Roman families and modern families were not quite the same. Here is a quotation from the writer Valerius Maximus: "Quintus Antistus Vetus divorced his wife because he had seen her talking in the street with some common women who were freed slaves." Like most societies today, Roman society was biased in favour of men—that is, men had much more power and authority than women. Part of this power was given to men by law, part by tradition. The law gave a man complete authority over the *familia*. Although the word looks like our word family it does not mean quite the same thing. It meant the family, in our sense of mother, father and children but also all other people and possessions in the house. Household might be a better word for *familia*. So the head of the family, the man, *owned* all that was in the house—wife, children, slaves and furniture.

The head of the family acted as the family priest and made sacrifices and offerings to the gods of the household. Women were not allowed to take part in public life at all, and certainly could not vote in elections.

Women's Rights?

Gradually, though, women got more power to act on their own and husbands lost the right to treat their wives as Vetus did. For example, there was a special form of marriage called *usus* in which a woman could avoid coming under the complete authority of her husband. A woman did have some power, of course, within the family as a

The tombstone of the woman Julia Velva found in Eboracum (now York). Notice the pine cones and remember (see page 65) how they were used. The scene shows the feast at Julia's funeral. Food is laid out on the little three-legged table while she reclines on a couch holding a glass. The inscription tells us that the man's name is Aurelius Mercurialis. Julia has left him her property and he may be her son-in-law married to the girl seated on the left. Perhaps the little boy is Julia's grandson. Tombstones give us a lot of evidence about the Romans. Look at the different furniture (table, two sorts of chair and a sofa), clothes (Aurelius has boots, cloak and a long-sleeved tunic) and hairstyles (the women have their hair parted in the middle and wear it over their ears). Try to work out some of the names in the Latin inscription. D M stands for DIS MANIBUS which means 'To the Gods of the Dead'.

mother and it was her job to run the domestic side of the household. She saw to the buying of food and essentials. Look, for example, at the woman in the butcher's shop on page 78. Women also went to the games and theatre, to the baths and to temples and processions to worship the gods. Of course, most of what you have just read applied mainly to wealthy families. Poor families did not have the choice of the wife staying at home in charge of a team of slaves!

A woman having her hair done, not at the hairdressers but by three of her household slaves—her maids. One is gathering the hair together, perhaps putting it into a bun like those of the maids themselves. Another is holding a flask—perhaps it's a hair dye or perfume. The other holds a polished bronze mirror. The drawing is taken from a sculpture found in Germany and was carved in the 3rd century AD.

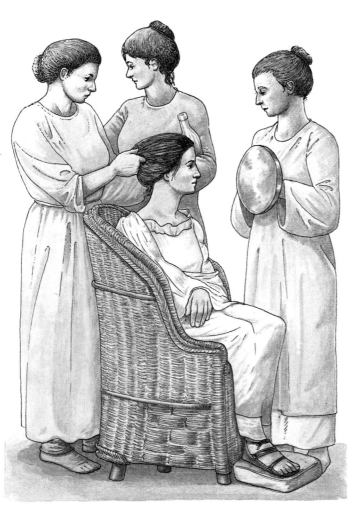

Children

In a letter from Egypt in 1 BC a soldier wrote to his wife, "If you give birth to a boy, keep it. If it's a girl, expose it. Try not to worry. As soon as we are paid I will send the money to you." It does seem extraordinary to us that parents were allowed to expose a new-born baby until it was dead. Some families simply could not afford to bring up children although various emperors did introduce family allowances for the poor to help them. In Roman society a boy was considered more useful than a girl. A boy could take part in public life, including the army, and had the protection of many more laws than girls did.

Both boys and girls were sent to school—at least for primary education (see page 69) but in well-to-do families girls were usually educated at home after that. There was no need for them to be prepared for a life outside the family. While a girl dedicated her toys to the gods of the household when she was married, a boy had a special ceremony when he was sixteen. He dedicated his *bulla* (the lucky charm he had worn around his neck since he was born) and his *toga praetexta* (a toga with a purple stripe). He was now officially a man and could wear the *toga virilis* or plain white toga worn by Roman citizens.

Household Slaves

The woman of the house was in charge of the children's upbringing and also of the slaves who worked as servants without pay. A number of slaves were needed to look after their owners and to keep the house running smoothly. Most slaves were probably treated quite well but, like the servants in the great English houses of the 18th and 19th centuries, they had to put up with the moods of their owners. The writer Juvenal reports: "If the mistress of the house is in a filthy mood because there is a curl out of place, then the slave girl who is doing her hair will have her own hair torn, her tunic ripped and she will be beaten with a strap."

Slaves were rewarded, though, as well as punished. A master or a mistress might allow them 'pocket money' and perhaps even set them free. This was often written into a person's will. A freed slave would then be a freedman, called a *libertus*, or a freedwoman—*liberta*. They did not have quite the same rights as citizens but their children became full citizens.

Toys and Games

Perhaps you are too old for toys like dolls or models. Did you know that Roman children had some of the same sorts of toy which children still play with today? Babies might have one of those 'squeaky animals'—a hollow model of a pig, perhaps, with a rattle inside. Miniature carts and horses have been found too.

We know that the Romans kept pets. Dogs were very common—you will often find them carved on tombstones. Look out for dog pawprints (and those of other animals) on tiles in museum collections. Cats were kept, too. Little figures of favourite animals (like the dog and mouse opposite) and of people were made. Below you can see a group of little pottery figures from a child's grave found in Colchester. It is probably a set used in a made-up dining room scene (see page 74). Some figures are reclining as if on couches. They are all concentrating on something and one is scratching his head. What are they looking at? The answer is in the figures at the back of the photograph. Some are reading from scrolls and the centre one appears to be speaking. They are probably entertaining the dinner guests by reading from a famous author or reciting a poem or part of a play. Can you imagine a Roman girl or boy setting out the figures in a make-believe game?

Dice and Board Games

Other indoor games played by children and adults involved dice, counters and a board like the one above. The dice could be used on their own. We

"I had a good win playing dice—and I didn't cheat!" Someone scribbled this on the wall of a bath-house in Pompeii. This board, counters, dice and shaker were found during the excavation of the Roman fort of Vindolanda on Hadrian's Wall.

know that they used the word *Venus* (the goddess) if they threw four sixes and the word *Canis* (dog) for the lowest score. A sort of dice game called *astragulus* used knucklebones and scores were kept for the different sides of the bones which landed face upwards. The two favourite games with boards were *Twelve Lines* which was a sort of backgammon game and *Robbers* where counters had different values and they had to take their opponents' pieces. *Robbers* was a favourite game for soldiers who introduced it to all parts of the Roman world.

For the more energetic there were outdoor games like wrestling or fencing or, more gently, bowling a hoop. Ball games were very popular. One was a bit like hockey which the Greeks also played. Another, called *trigon*, involved three people in a triangle quickly throwing hard leather balls to one another. Another was called *harpastum* and involved trying to snatch away a heavy ball—perhaps a bit like rugby.

School

"As soon as his son was old enough, Cato took him in hand and taught him to read even though he had a good slave, called Chilo, who was a schoolteacher and taught many other boys. So Cato himself taught his son reading and writing, the law and gymnastics, and all sorts of outdoor skill such as throwing a javelin, fighting in armour, horse riding, boxing, swimming and how to stand up to heat and cold."

Plutarch.

Cato was an important politician and writer who was born in 234 BC. Many Romans would have considered it 'old fashioned' not to have used an educated slave to teach their children. Usually by the age of seven children were sent out of the home to school. The schoolmaster, called the *magister ludi,* took a small number of paying pupils. He might set up a school in his home or rent a room somewhere. Lessons began at dawn but finished in the early afternoon. The teachers were usually very strict and would beat their pupils with a cane or strap if they did not attend or learn their lessons.

In the picture below you can see some boys at school. The teacher has a scroll on his lap, as some of the boys have. These scrolls, with writing on, were the Roman equivalent of books but were made of papyrus.

Two small bronze figures which were probably played with as toys. The mouse is from a grave in York and the dog was found at Hadrian's Wall.

They wrote on the scrolls with pens and ink. Can you spot the inkwell? Two boys are using wax tablets to write on. They are edged boards of wood with wax poured inside. You could scratch the letters on them with a *stylus*—a sharp point made of metal or bone. You could also scratch the letters off and use the wax again—just like a blackboard or the slates children used in the 19th century.

Secondary School

After five years at this first school, children went on to a secondary school. There they were taught by a master called a *grammaticus*. The children learnt about Greek and Latin literature, history, arithmetic, geometry and astronomy. Some pupils, usually boys, went on to complete their education abroad. Greece was a favourite place to go for a sort of university education with special teachers.

Clothes and Fashion

We have a lot of evidence for the way Roman people looked and for their clothes and their jewellery. Statues, like the one of Julius Caesar on page 30, usually give us details of hairstyles. Carving on tombs, like the one on page 66, may provide evidence for different types of clothes. As you look through this book notice the people's faces—you may see a Roman looking like someone you know!

Clothes

People wore underclothes as we do today. Round your waist you tied a *subligaculum* or loincloth. Women also wore a breast band (or brassière) called a

strophium. In colder parts of the Roman world men sometimes wore trousers, called *bracae*, which were skin tight and stretched down to the ankles. Men, women and children wore tunics over their underclothes. These were usually gathered at the waist if they were to be seen. A woman might wear an undertunic and then a long tunic or *stola* like the drawing on the left. It is gathered at the waist and again just below the bust with a belt of some sort. Even though the shape of the women's stola remained the same for practically the entire Roman period, certain materials and colours were fashionable at different times. Tunics and stolas (of wool, linen and silk) came in a variety of colours—white, black, yellow, green, blue, red, purple, in all sorts of shades.

The Toga

The outer garment you can see the man on the left wearing is called a *toga*. A toga was a sign of being a Roman citizen so not everyone was allowed to wear one. It was a very large, loose piece of clothing but extremely comfortable. You can see the first stages of putting on a toga on the far right but the man here has tucked his around his waist—there was a lot of cloth to deal with! Both the man and the woman are wearing leather sandals, which came in a variety of styles.

Left: Typical clothes for a well-to-do Roman couple. Look for other examples of clothing, hairstyles and shoes elsewhere in the book.
Below: Jewellery was popular with women and men. Look for brooches, rings, necklaces, earrings and hairpins on other illustrations in the book. People kept their jewellery and other valuables in wooden boxes. This is a ring with a key attached—a good way not to lose your key!

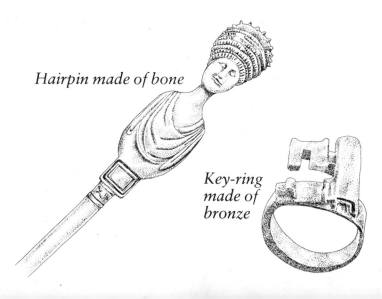

Hairpin made of bone

Key-ring made of bronze

The Palla

For outdoor wear the woman would have a loose fitting *palla*. It was really a very large shawl, rectangular in shape, which could cover her entire body and be draped over the head as well. Men and women wore cloaks of various sorts, either tied or fastened with a brooch at the neck. Sometimes cloaks had hoods like the ploughman's on page 86. Knitted socks or stockings made of cloth were also worn in cold weather.

Hairstyles

Men and women took a good deal of trouble over their hair. Most men were clean-shaven up to the 2nd century AD when beards became popular. Women's hairstyles were sometimes fairly simple, like the one on the left from Roman Egypt but could take a long time to arrange—see how many slaves are in attendance on page 67. Sometimes hair might be held in place by a thin hairnet, called a *reticulum*, and long pins. Women dyed their hair—blonde and red were favourite colours. Wigs, made with the hair of captured blondes from Germany or dark-haired women from India, were often used.

Women used make-up—chalk for a white skin, red ochre for lips and cheeks and perhaps ashes for darkening the eyebrows. Sets of instruments for plucking hairs, cleaning the ears and applying make-up and perfume are often found in excavations of Roman sites.

Right: The toga *was made of a single piece of cloth—wool, linen or even silk if you could afford it. As the drawing (1) shows it was semi-circular in shape. Its width was usually three times the height of the person. You might make one out of an old sheet. To wear it, drape one end (2) over your left shoulder so that it reaches your ankle. Pass the other end (3) under your right arm and across your left shoulder where it could be pinned with a brooch.*

A Roman Home

Houses

In Roman towns the house you lived in depended on how wealthy you were. If you were rich your house would have a large number of rooms, perhaps twenty or thirty, for your family and your house-slaves. Because the Romans liked to be as private as possible inside their houses, they often had no windows on the outside walls, at least downstairs. This also made burglary difficult. Roman town houses had no front gardens and the front door was on the street or just inside an entrance passageway. In the passageway of the house below visitors would find a strange welcome. It was the mosaic you can see on page 83 of a ferocious dog. The dog, if there was one, would be looked after by the doorman who kept unwelcome or uninvited visitors away. To make the house even more private and to keep the living areas well away from the noisy street, the front two rooms were often rented out as shops, as here.

Inside the House

Let's see what the house was like inside. Once past the doorman you would be standing in the *atrium*—the hall. This was a large two-storey room with an enormous skylight. This let in the much needed light for the bedrooms and living rooms around the hall. Where the light could come in through the roof the rain also came in, and so immediately below was an ornamental pool, called an *impluvium*. This part of the House of the Tragic Poet had two storeys with bedrooms above for both the family and the house-slaves. Notice that they have separate staircases (and that the slaves' staircase is narrower) just as in English houses in the 18th and 19th centuries, when people had servants.

Below: This Pompeian house was given the name of the House of the Tragic Poet by the archaeologists who uncovered it because the wall paintings and mosaics showed scenes from tragedies performed at the theatre. The mosaic on page 58 is from the main living room of this house.

KEY

1 Entrance passage
2 Shops
3 Staircase for family
4 Staircase for servants
5 Hall
6 Rainwater basin
7 Bedrooms
8 Side rooms
9 Living room
10 Passageway
11 Small living room
12 Garden courtyard
13 Kitchen
14 Dining room
15 Back door

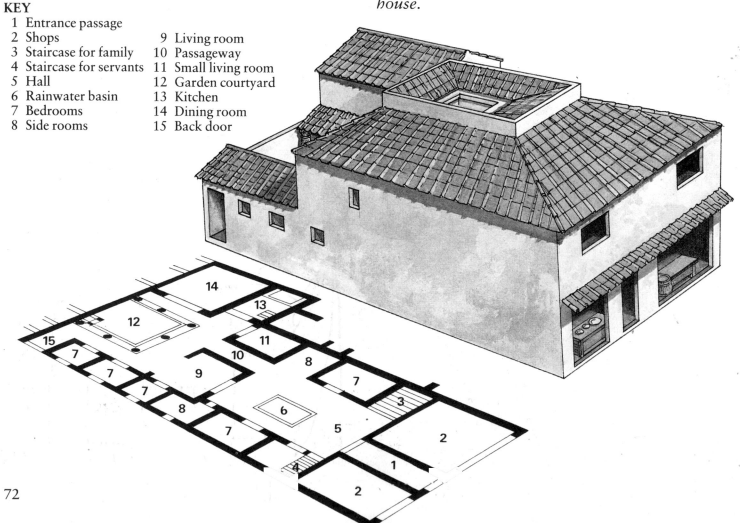

The most important room in the house was the *tablinum*—the main living room. It was open to the hall and the garden by means of hinged or sliding wooden doors, or just curtains. Notice the passageway on the plan of the house which allows the slaves to pass through into the garden or kitchen without disturbing the family in the living room.

Garden, Dining room and Kitchen

The garden is similar (though smaller) to the one in the House of the Vetii Brothers below. There is a roofed colonnade or *peristyle* around the garden itself. In one corner, near the back door, was the *lararium*. This was a little shrine for the gods who looked after this household. On the right-hand side of the garden was the *triclinium*—the dining room. It must have been pleasant to eat looking out over the quiet enclosed garden. In just the right place next to the dining room was the *culina*—the kitchen.

Flats

"We live in a city shored up with slender props—for that's how the landlords stop the houses from falling down."

Juvenal.

The writer Juvenal complained about the ramshackle buildings the poor had to live in. They were blocks—*insulae*—with a number of flats and

Blocks of flats at Ostia, the port of Rome, with shops at street level. Some of those living in these flats would have been shopkeepers.

single rooms for people to rent. In Rome these blocks of flats were five or six storeys high but in towns where there was more room, such as Pompeii and Ostia, they were usually only two or three storeys. The flats at Ostia (above) are strongly built of brick but many in Rome were of wood and plaster and built very close together. They frequently burnt to the ground.

The garden, with its small trees, shrubs and herbs for the kitchen, at the back of the House of the Vetii Brothers, rich merchants. An open corridor of columns provided a cool pleasant walkway and protected the rooms around from bad weather. Here you would find bedrooms and a triclinium. This house had several dining rooms, placed to catch the light at different times of the year. Wall paintings of garden scenes help archaeologists to reconstruct what one sort of garden might have looked like. This garden has been replanted in the original beds. There were also several fountains—all connected to a water supply by underground lead pipes.

Cooking

The Romans usually had three meals a day. As soon as it was light the family would rise to eat a breakfast, called *ientaculum,* of bread and fruit. At midday, there was usually a light meal, *prandium,* of cold meat, fish, vegetables and bread. The main meal of the day was called the *cena* and began around four o'clock in the afternoon. Its various courses could go on until well into the evening.

The main meal was divided into three courses. First was the *gustatio*—literally a taster—which was a variety of dishes made from eggs or fish or vegetables. Oysters were very popular, as were snails which were fattened on milk. Stuffed dormice might be part of this taster course. The wine served with the *gustatio* was mixed with honey and called *mulsum.*

The main course, called *primae mensae,* had roast or boiled meats and poultry. Often these dishes were plain, such as sausages or stew but sometimes, for special occasions, they were exotic—such as boiled ostrich! Ordinary wine was drunk, often mixed with water. The meal finished with the *secundae mensae* when sweets and fruit were usually served.

Of course not all Roman families had a great choice for the main meal every day. If you were rich enough, though, and had lots of house-slaves it was easy to provide a great variety of food. If you were poor, what you ate would have been simpler and would have contained little meat or fish. Your diet would have consisted of a lot of bread, stews of vegetables and a sort of porridge or gruel made from barley and wheat.

Below: The Roman name for the dining room was triclinium. *The name comes from the way the dining room was usually arranged—three couches forming three sides of a square. The diners recline, taking food from low tables kept stocked from the kitchen by house-slaves. Above you can see the cook preparing the next courses, surrounded by pots and pans. Every kitchen had a* mortarium *for grinding up the spices used in Roman cooking.*

Lots of Flavours

You will see from the recipes below how many different sorts of flavourings the Romans liked to add to their food. They used lots of herbs which could easily be grown such as coriander, oregano, mint, thyme, fennel and sage. They also imported spices from the eastern parts of the Empire, and beyond, from places like India. The most important of these spices was pepper but they also liked nutmeg, cloves, cardamom and ginger, for example. Roman cooks also used specially prepared sauces—various wine sauces and one called *liquamen* made from salted fish and fish insides left to become liquid in the sun. Many Roman dishes seem too spicy for our tastes today but it was a good way to disguise the flavour of food which was bad or cover up the taste of the metal pots and pans they used—some of them made from lead.

A Roman Recipe Book

The recipes given on this page are from Marcus Apicius' recipe book. The recipes date from the 1st century AD. You might like to try some of them (not the dormice, please!) but watch out for the honey—if you are not careful it will burn in the frying pan.

Cabbages with Leeks

"Put the boiled cabbages into a shallow saucepan and season with liquamen, oil, ordinary wine and cumin. Sprinkle with pepper, leeks, caraway seeds and fresh coriander."

This dish could be cooked in an oven to bring out the flavour of all the ingredients or eaten cold—like a salad—with a meat dish.

Stuffed Dormice

The Romans were very fond of dormice—to eat— and thought they were a great delicacy. The dormice were force-fed on nuts in specially-made clay pots with air holes.

"Stuff dormice with minced pork and also whole minced dormice which have been pounded with pepper, pine-kernels, asafoetida and liquamen. Sew up the dormice and put them on a tile in the oven."

Home-made Sweets

"Stuffed dates: Stone the dates and stuff with nuts, pine kernels or ground pepper. Roll them in salt and fry in warmed honey, then serve."

"Honeyed bread: Remove crust from a wholewheat loaf and break into largish pieces. Soak them in milk, fry in oil, then pour honey over and serve."

"Sweets: Take the best wheat flour and cook in boiling water or milk until it becomes a stiff paste. Spread it onto a plate and when cold cut it up for sweets and fry in the best oil. Remove from the oil and pour honey over them, sprinkle with pepper and serve."

In the Street

The areas where most people lived were also where the shops, offices and workshops were. In four of the districts in Rome where records of the number of buildings survive, there were 30 blocks of flats for every one private house. Several writers complained about the noise. Juvenal said:

"How can anyone sleep in lodgings here? It's only the rich who get any sleep. The noise of the carts thundering along the narrow streets and the language of the drivers when they get stuck in a traffic jam would wake even the heaviest sleeper."

The reason for all this noise at night was that a law forbade any carts coming into the city for ten hours after daybreak. The only exception to this was those carrying building materials. Towns and cities, especially Rome, always had some district being redeveloped.

Even with this traffic law the streets were very busy from dawn onwards. Juvenal, again, has something to say about this:

"However fast we hurry there's a huge crowd ahead and a mob behind pushing and shoving. You get dug in the ribs by someone's elbow. Then someone hits you with a long pole, another with a beam from a building or a wine-barrel. The streets are filthy—our legs are plastered with mud, someone tramples your feet or a soldier's

EVERYDAY LIFE

hob-nailed boot lands right on your toe. Togas which have just been patched are torn. A great trunk of a fir tree sways in its rumbling waggon and totters menacingly over the heads of the crowd."

At the Baker's

There were many bakers in towns as bread formed a major part of people's diet. The reconstruction below is of one found at Pompeii. A *pistrinum*—the Roman name for a bakery—was the place where all the processes in making bread were carried out. On the right you can see the great millstones made out of volcanic lava-stone. The stone is very hard but also rough so that it can easily grind the wheat into flour. The millstones were turned by slaves, donkeys or oxen. At the back of the shop the flour is made into dough and baked in the ovens. Bread was sold, all hot and fresh, from the counter which faces the street. A notice outside probably advertised the bread.

Over the oven of one of Pompeii's many bakeries someone has written, "On the 1st of April I made bread". Odd really, as bread must have been baked there at least twice a day. The bakery shown in the 19th-century drawing on page 46 had all the lunchtime supplies in the oven when it was uncovered.

Shops

There were no supermarkets in Roman towns, of course, but lots of different shops making and selling all sorts. Plautus lists in one of his plays a clothes-cleaner, haberdasher, wool-seller, jeweller, dyers, shoemakers, weavers, lace-sellers and cabinet makers. There were plenty of food shops as well as butchers, grocers and greengrocers. Shopkeepers had to put up with competition from street vendors. The poet Martial talks about sellers of pease-pudding, salt and sausages carrying their trays along the busy streets.

Roman Take-aways

Many people who lived in a single room or small flat often had no means of cooking their own food. Where flats were made of wood people were forbidden by law to cook in the building—though many did, which is why there were so many fires in towns. People were forced to go out to eat or bring home 'take-aways'. You would not have to search far for a take-away, *thermopolium,* in a Roman town. They were easy to spot, too, by the rows of containers sunk into the counters for the hot snacks.

A *thermopolium* might smell quite nice from the street but some food producers, or other small industries, must have been the source of rather strong smells. Not many people would have been happy about living near a *liquamen* producer, for instance.

A jar found at Pompeii had this inscription on it, "The best strained liquamen from the factory of Umbricius Agathopus". Liquamen was made in the following way: the gills, blood and intestines of fish; as well as whole small fish, were put into an open jar with salt. Wine, various sweet herbs and vinegar was added and the mixture was left in the sun until it had become a liquid. This took two or three months. This very strongly flavoured fish sauce could then be put into jars and sold.

Shops at Pompeii

Quite often shops advertised themselves with signs, such as legs of pork outside a butcher's, or notices painted on the outside wall like this one from Pompeii, "Zosimus sells pots, particularly for liquamen". On the right you can see one of the streets in Pompeii lined with shops, but not at all like ours today. Roman shops were not enclosed with a door and glass front. In the morning the shopkeeper would remove from the front of the

Below: A Roman woman waiting for her order to be prepared at the butcher's shop. She is holding her shopping list on her lap written on a wax tablet. The butcher has a range of cuts of meat and a steelyard or balance for weighing them out for the customers. Notice the three-legged chopping block. See if you can spot one in a modern butcher's.

The tomb of a rich baker in Rome called Zethus. On the left is a millstone and on the right a sieve and various sizes of measure for flour and bread moulds.

shop wooden panels which had been padlocked to a stone sill on the pavement. You can often see the groove where the panels fitted. Just inside was a counter, very often L-shaped. Containers were set into the surface and, if it was a hot food shop, a fire burned underneath. If the shopkeeper was a wine or oil merchant then you would expect to find large *amphorae* storing the produce in a back room.

Weights and Measures

We saw on page 48 that one of the buildings around the *forum* at Pompeii was the office for the weights and measures department. Inspectors went to shops and workshops to check on what was being sold. Here are some Roman weights and measures and the modern equivalents:

Libra—the Roman pound weight (327·45 grammes) which was divided into 12 unciae (ounces).

Sextarius—mainly used as a measure for liquid but was also for measuring corn (0·96 of a pint).

Amphora—was not only a type of storage jar but also a measure of volume. It equalled 25·79 litres or 5·67 gallons.

Pes—the Roman foot which measures 29·46 centimetres.

Mille passuum—the Roman mile (1475 metres), just short of the English mile.

Shops and workshops lining one of the streets in Pompeii. "Before it gets light we have the bakers, then it's the hammering of the coppersmiths all day."
Martial

Crafts and Trades

We saw on page 44 the great variety of goods traded all over the Roman world. In towns the businesses, industries and shops served the people of the town and the countryside around. Some goods for sale were brought to the town from farms, some were imported (such as silks from the East) and some were made in factories in the town itself.

You might find whole streets given over to a particular craft or trade—leather goods or furniture making, for instance. In the Roman world factories were not large establishments, as they often are today, employing a great many people. Workshops might be a better word for them. Even so some crafts required a number of workers. For example, to operate a pottery or tile works you would need workers to dig and prepare the clay, to make the products, mix glazes, build and fire the kilns, store and transport the finished products. A shoemaker, on the other hand, might work on his own or with a few apprentices—his workshop inside the shop itself on the street. Let's look at three crafts in more detail.

The Tile-maker

"Tiles or bricks should be made in the spring or in the autumn, so that they can dry straight away. When the sun is too strong it overbakes the skin of the tile which makes it seem dry but really the inside is not properly dried."

Vitruvius, the architect, is writing here about sun-dried bricks which were used in some parts of the Roman world together with stone and wood in building. The Romans turned to firing tiles in a kiln to make them withstand the weather. The Romans used an enormous number of fired tiles, of all sorts, in their buildings. Tileworks often had their own stamps on batches of tiles and there were a number of towns which ran their own tile factories.

What sorts of tile did the tilemaker have to produce for the builders? The largest type was probably the flat roof tile called the *tegula*. You can see from the drawing below that it had flanges on each side. It was quite large, measuring about 1 by 1½ Roman feet. These overlapped all over the roof and were covered by a half-round tile called an *imbrex*. The *imbrex* was also used for the ridge of the roof. To finish off the ends of the lines of these half-round tiles they used *antefixa*—triangular shaped tiles, sometimes with a decoration on. Plain flat tiles, roughly the size of a *tegula*, were used in various parts of a building. They might be used on the floor and in wall building to form a flat surface, or as courses or lines in a stone wall.

If you look back to page 52 you will see another type of tile in use. We have seen how the floor of the hot room was raised to allow the *hypocaust* heating to work. The pillars were made from thick square tiles called *pilae*. Can you see where our word pillar comes from? To take the heat from under the floor special box tiles were made to act

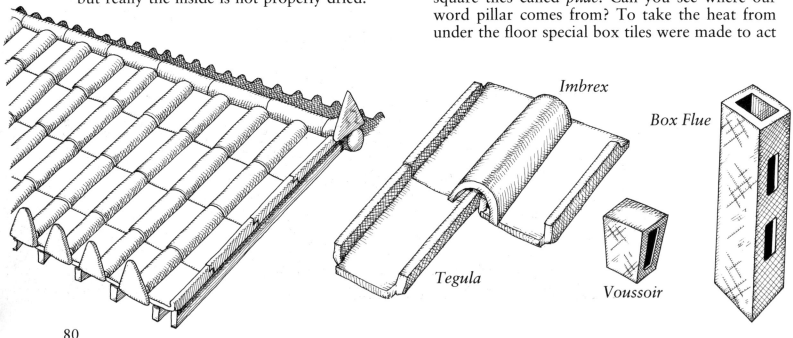

Imbrex

Box Flue

Tegula

Voussoir

as an air flue. There is a drawing of one on page 80. Put on top of one another they formed a squarish pipe which went from under the floor to the roof. The face of the tile has markings on it—either made by hand or by a special roller—to help the mortar and plaster to stick to it. If you needed hot air to pass right over a room (as in the baths on page 52) you used a *voussoir* tile.

Many tiles for the workers to make, but not all the workers worked all the time. One workman at a tile factory in London scratched his complaint about a fellow-worker on a tile waiting to go into the kiln, "Austalis has been skiving off by himself every day for the last 13 days".

The Builder

On the right, in a wall painting from Rome, you can see builders at work on a wall of stone. Notice that the stone is cut into regular blocks, with the *face* or outside edge smooth. Since the Romans hadn't invented explosives, large blocks of stone, such as marble, had to be hacked, hammered and sawn out of quarries. Stone was brought into large towns from many different parts of the Roman world. The blocks in this painting are being *mortared* together with a mixture of sand and lime. The man in the foreground is carrying wet mortar in a basket to his fellow workers.

There was a great need for builders in all Roman towns. There were not only new public buildings (such as temples and market halls) but also private houses and flats to build and repair. Look out for different types of construction, especially using stone tiles, elsewhere in the book.

The Blacksmith

The Romans never discovered how to make *cast* iron—that is, melted iron ore poured into a mould. The Roman blacksmith had to heat up the iron ore and beat out the shape of the object on an anvil. You can see what went on at the blacksmith's from the sculpture below. It is from the tomb of a blacksmith. On the left his assistant is heating up the forge with bellows and is shielded from the intense heat of the fire. In the middle sits the blacksmith himself with his apron across his tunic. He is holding the object to be made with his tongs and is beating it with a hammer on the anvil. On the right the tools of his trade are carved large and also some of the things he specializes in—a spearhead and a door-lock.

Wall Paintings and Mosaics

We know from the evidence which has survived that those Romans who could afford houses liked to have as much of them decorated as possible. Floors, walls and ceilings had paintings or mosaics on them. Roman artists also produced paintings, and small mosaics, to hang on the wall or stand on an easel in a room.

There were a number of different subjects to choose from, depending on the room the decoration was to go in. There was often a 'still life'— perhaps a bowl of fruit and a wine glass—in the dining room. In the main living room there might be a series of scenes—perhaps from the theatre or from traditional stories about gods and heroes. Decoration inside houses often tells us a lot about crafts and trades, as we have already seen. You will find this sort of decoration in shops, offices (see page 44), temples and bath-houses, too.

All over the Roman world there were patterns and designs which were popular. Artists carried pattern books with them for their clients to choose a new wall or floor decoration.

Wall Painting

"When the plastered walls are made solid and have been polished like white marble they will look splendid after the colours are put on. When the colours are carefully put on to wet plaster they do not fade but become permanent."

Vitruvius.

Vitruvius tells us that several layers of plaster had to be applied to the walls to make a hard smooth surface. The technique of painting described above is *fresco* painting—that is, where the paint is applied before the last skim of plaster has dried. There were plenty of colours to choose from. Red and yellow could be taken from ochre, green from green earth, black from carbon or soot, white from chalk. Some colours were quite expensive to produce—blue from a glass and copper mixture, purple from certain sea shells. You can see some of these very bright colours in the painting on the right. This is part of a larger landscape scene—a subject the Romans were very fond of. In the room on the far right painters are finishing off the wall panels.

Mosaics

The most extraordinary form of interior decoration to survive from the Roman world was the mosaic floor. You can see them in most museums in Europe which have Roman collections. A mosaic floor was made of very small cubes, called *tesserae*, of stone or tile laid in mortar. Plain coloured floors, simple designs or complicated pictures could all be made by the skilful mosaic-maker. There is a fairly simple one of a dog on the right but you have seen others in the book. Look back to page 58 for a very detailed theatre picture, all of stone.

The more the mosaic-maker wanted his work to appear like a painting, the smaller the *tesserae* had to be. Very large numbers of the little cubes would

Part of a wall painting from the town of Stabiae which was destroyed by the volcano Vesuvius along with Pompeii and Herculaneum.

CRAFTS AND TRADES

be needed—about 15 million to lay a 15 m square floor! Mosaic-makers, like those below, had several apprentices or slaves to cut the stone for them. Sometimes the central picture of a mosaic floor would be made up in the workshop and carried to the house. These ready-made mosaic floors could be sold for export to various places in the Roman world.

Suetonius wrote, "It is recorded that Julius Caesar carried mosaics with him on his campaigns". You can see how keen the Romans were on their interior decoration!

Right: This mosaic is from the front entrance of the house in Pompeii shown on page 72. The words underneath, CAVE CANEM, mean 'Beware of the Dog'. It did not always mean there was a guard dog inside (some mosaics show a ferocious bear!) but it did mean that passers-by were not encouraged to come in.

Life in the Country

On a Roman Villa

When a Roman used the word *villa* it meant a number of things. It could mean a grand house in the country, sometimes with a farming estate attached to it. It might mean a holiday house in the countryside, near the mountains or by the sea. It might mean a simple farmhouse.

To build a pleasant holiday home or a grand estate house the owner needed to make a good profit from his farms. Much of the produce from farms was sold at local markets in towns but some was exported to other parts of the Roman world and especially to Rome.

The reconstruction drawing (right) shows part of a large *villa*. It is based on evidence of villas from Gaul. We also know quite a lot about farms, farm buildings and agriculture from Roman writers. Lucius Columella, in about 60 AD, wrote a farming 'textbook' called *About Farming*. In it he describes what a proper *villa* should be:

"A farm should be in a healthy climate, with fertile soil, with some flat ground and some hilly on an eastern or southern slope, which is not too steep. The villa should have three sections; the *villa urbana*—that is the house of the owner, the *villa rustica*—the house of the farm manager and labourers and the *villa fructuaria*—the store-house."

The Buildings

Look for the house of the owner on the right. It is rather grand with laid-out gardens and its own bath-house (on the left—see the smoke coming from the roof). Notice the wall which divides the *villa urbana* from the farmyard.

"The *villa rustica* should have a high kitchen … little rooms for slaves who are not kept chained and for those who are chained there should be an underground prison, as healthy a place as is possible. For the cattle there should be stables which can be used in both hot and cold weather. Rooms for the herdsmen and shepherds should be next to the animals they look after."

Where is the *villa rustica*? Look for a building (with its own little garden) which is rather like the owner's house but not as grand. Elsewhere in the farmyard are the various buildings which make up the *villa fructuaria*. Columella says this should "have rooms for oil, for the presses, for wine … hay-lofts … granaries … on the ground floor storage for wine and oil to be taken to market".

Look below for the great pottery storage jars set into the ground in their own walled area, well away from the trample of farm animals and carts. It was into these containers which went the *villa*'s produce of oil or wine.

S.BIESTY

Working on the Land

Where did all the wealth come from to enable a fine house to be built for the owner, or even one for the farm manager? By hard work, especially by the hard work of the farmworkers who were usually slaves. Life was very hard for most of them. In fact slaves who tried to escape or who were troublesome were chained together—even when they were working.

The day-to-day running of the farm was looked after by the *vilicus*, the farm manager. He might be a slave himself but he needed to know a lot about farming and controlling the workers. He was in charge and had to answer to his master if the farm didn't show a profit. Columella says the *vilicus* "must be someone who has been hardened by farm-work since childhood and tested by practical experience". Another writer, Marcus Cato, says this of the *vilicus*;

Left: From a bronze model, only 5 cm high, of a ploughman with two oxen. Found in Piercebridge, County Durham in Britain, it was perhaps made in Gaul in the 2nd or 3rd century AD.
"Some land, when you have ploughed it with oxen and plough, must be ploughed again before you plant the seed." *Marcus Varro.*

Right: From a mosaic floor in a villa in southern Gaul—the olive harvest has begun. The olives will be taken back to the villa for pressing into oil and stored for eating and for sale.
"When the olives are ripe they should be picked as soon as possible. Do not allow them to remain on the floor of the storehouse for long. The sooner you begin to mill them the better the results will be." *Marcus Cato.*

Left: From a 3rd century AD *tomb in Rome. A farmworker is milking a goat into a clay pot.*
"Cheese should be made of pure milk which is as fresh as possible. Some mix in crushed green pine-kernels and curdle it, but you can make different flavoured cheese by adding any seasoning you like." *Lucius Columella.*

LIFE IN THE COUNTRY

"The farm manager must not be an idler, he must always be sober and must not go out to dine. He must be the first to rise in the morning and last to bed. Before that he must see that the farm is shut up and that everyone is asleep in the right place and that the animals have fodder."

A *vilica* or housekeeper was in charge inside the house and of all the household slaves. She would probably also be a slave and may have been the wife of the *vilicus*. Cato says of her, "She must be clean herself and keep the farm clean and neat. She must clean and tidy the fire-place every night before she goes to bed."

There were a great number of different jobs to be done each day by the farmworkers. Some would spend most of their time with animals or seeing to the growing of crops. There were always jobs to be done on repairing tools, machinery and farm buildings. The *vilicus* would need to make sure he had workers who were skilful enough to do maintenance. For some jobs, such as that of the blacksmith or pottery making, specialist firms would have to be brought in.

Right: A harvesting machine called a vallus *from a sculpture found in the province of Gallia Belgica at Buzenol, now in Luxembourg. It is pushed by a donkey or by oxen and the machine cuts the crop down.*
"In the vast estates in Gaul a very large machine called a vallus with teeth at the edge and carried on two wheels is driven through the corn." *Pliny.*

Left: Sacks of grapes being brought from the vineyard. From a mosaic floor in a house in Augusta, now Paphos, the Roman capital of the island of Cyprus.
"Get everything ready that is needed for making the wine. Wash out the vats and repair the baskets. Gather the not-so-good grapes for the coarse wine for the workers to drink." *Marcus Cato.*

Right: From a 1st century BC tomb in Germany. It shows a farmer taking produce to market past a roadside shrine.
"If there are towns or villages in the neighbourhood, or even rich estates, from which you can buy what you need for the farm . . . you can sell your surplus." *Marcus Varro.*

How It All Ended

If you look back to the map of the Roman world (on page 7) as it was in the 2nd century AD you will see one of the problems in establishing Roman power and a Roman way of life. The major problem was that the Empire was so large. At its borders were people who were ready to attack and take over Roman territory. By the 3rd century AD some parts of the Roman Empire were already suffering from these attacks. For example, the Goths came down from Russia and rampaged through Greece and captured Athens in AD 267.

Splitting the Empire

The Romans tried to deal with the problem of controlling such a large Empire by dividing it into two parts. In AD 330 the Emperor Constantine established an imperial palace in Constantinople (now Istanbul in Turkey). After the reign of the Emperor Theodosius I the Empire was ruled by two quite separate emperors—one based in Rome, the other in Constantinople.

The Emperor Diocletian built this palace at Spalato (now Split in Yugoslavia) between AD 300 and 306, for his retirement, near the place where he had been born. The outline of the square palace remains with its gates and guard towers as well as some of the palace buildings inside. The palace, covering 39,000 square metres, was really a small fortified town for the emperor, showing how threatened people felt in the Roman world in the 4th century AD. Almost half the area was taken up with barracks for soldiers. In the half nearest the sea were splendid palace buildings including a temple, a mausoleum *(elaborate building for burial), a basilica and a baths.*

HOW IT ALL ENDED

A gold coin showing the Emperor Justinianus. It was minted to celebrate his general Belisarius' defeat of the vandals in AD 535.

The Western Empire

The western part of the Empire really suffered from the attacks of those the Romans called *barbari*—the barbarians.

For example:

AD 376 Visigoths (from western Russia) cross the River Danube.

AD 409 Vandals (from Hungary) and Visigoths begin to invade Europe.

AD 429 Vandals take over north Africa.

The last Roman emperor in the west, called Romulus Augustulus, only reigned from AD 475 to 476. Odovacar, who led German armies in Italy, took over and declared himself king. The 'barbarians' were now in control of the Western Empire.

On the Edges of the Empire

"We have planted our crops only for the enemy to burn. All our resources are gone— the flocks of sheep, the herds of camels and horses. I am writing this behind walls, under siege."

A Christian bishop called Synesius wrote this in the early years of the 5th century AD when his province of Cyrenaica in northern Africa was being overrun by 'barbarians'. Roman control was rapidly breaking down. There were few, if any, soldiers to protect the countryside against invasion. People retreated into towns which had strong walls.

Invasions of new peoples did not mean that 'Roman' life disappeared completely. In many areas it was simply adapted by the newcomers. Archaeological evidence for this process is shown below. It is from the town of Wroxeter (see pages 10–13) on the western side of Rome's most northerly province—Britain. Britain's south and east coasts were hard pressed by invasions of Saxons from the continent in the 5th century. Yet on the borders of Wales 400 km away the evidence points to a Roman-style redevelopment of the town. By the 6th century, however, most traces of Roman life will probably have disappeared.

The Eastern Empire

The eastern part of the Empire was not as hard pressed by the *barbari*. From the capital at Constantinople it controlled territory as far away as Greece in the west, Egypt and Cyrenaica in the south and the borders of Arabia in the east. The Emperor Justinianus reconquered lands lost to the Vandals in Africa, to the Ostrogoths in Italy and to the Visigoths in southern Spain. It was a good attempt at re-establishing the old idea of a full Roman empire but gradually land was lost in the west again. Italy was lost to the Lombards (from across the River Danube) in AD 568 and in the next century Africa and Spain were taken over by the Muslims. The Holy Roman Empire—Constantinople had been Christian since its foundation—continued to be ruled by emperors until AD 1453 when its capital fell to the Ottoman Turks.

At Wroxeter new town houses in Roman-style architecture were being constructed entirely of wood in a grand redevelopment of the city centre in the 5th century AD.

BC	
753	Legend says Rome was founded by Romulus.
	Republic established
509	Romans throw out their Etruscan kings and establish the Republic
449	The Sabines are finally conquered.
about 400	The Gauls look for new land in Italy.
390	The Gauls occupy Rome. Sacred geese save Capitol Hill.
343–290	Samnite Wars.
	War with Carthage
264–241	First War with Carthage
247	Hannibal born.
237–202	Second War with Carthage.
221	Hannibal in command of forces in Spain.
218	Crossing of the Alps.
202	Hannibal's forces finally defeated at Battle of Zama.
about 190	Plautus' play *The Rope* first performed.
183	Hannibal commits suicide.
149–146	Third War against Carthage. The new province of Africa established.
133–122	*Land reforms* of Gaius and Tiberius Gracchus.
106	Cicero, the orator, born.

BC	
	Marius versus Sulla
86	Marius died.
81–80	Sulla dictator.
78	Sulla died.
	Julius Caesar
73	His first political office.
60	Consul.
59–49	Conquered Gaul and invaded Britain twice.
	Civil War
49	No turning back for Caesar— he crosses the Rubicon.
48	Pompey murdered.
45	Caesar defeats the remains of Pompey's forces at the Battle of Munda.
44	Caesar becomes Dictator for Life and is murdered.
	War with Antony
31	Senate declares war on Cleopatra. Octavianus defeats Antony at the Battle of Actium.
29	Octavianus declares peace in the Roman world.
	The Empire
27	Octavianus becomes Augustus the Emperor.
before 27	Vitruvius, the architect, writes his manuals.

THE ROMAN CALENDAR

AD	
11	Livy finishes his 142 volumes of the *History of Rome*.
14	Augustus died.
37	Josephus, the historian, born.
about 40	The poet Martial born.
43	Emperor Claudius invades Britain.
about 60	Columella writes *About Farming*.
61	Pliny, the politician and writer, born.
73	Romans besiege Masada.
79	Vesuvius erupts—Pompeii destroyed.
80	Emperor Titus opens the world's largest amphitheatre, the Colosseum.
114	Emperor Trajan builds his column in Rome.
121	Suetonius' *Lives of the Emperors* published.
122	Emperor Hadrian visits Britain. Hadrian's Wall begun.
212	All men in the provinces are made Roman citizens.
267	Goths capture Athens.
286	Carausius proclaimed Emperor after 26 emperors in 50 years.
300–306	Emperor Diocletian builds his fortified palace at Split.
330	Emperor Constantine moves the capital from Rome. Byzantium becomes Constantinople.
409	Vandals begin to invade Europe.
475–6	Romulus Augustulus the last emperor in the west.

Eastern Empire

535	Belisarius, Emperor Justinianus' general, defeats Vandals.
1453	Turks capture Constantinople. Fall of the Holy Roman Empire.

Even before the Etruscans took over Rome a calendar was in use. It was based on the phases of the moon and was divided into ten months, later twelve months. The year had 355 days in it. To make the length of the year right they added an extra month of 22 or 23 days every two years. The Roman year began on March 1st at first, but later, in 153 BC, it was changed to January 1st.

By the time of Julius Caesar the calendar was in chaos because no extra month had been added since 58 BC. This meant that the Roman year was now 90 days too short! Caesar decided to do something about the calendar and made some changes in 46 BC. He declared the year to have 365 days in it. Actually he knew that it was slightly longer than that and so added an extra day to February every fourth year—our Leap Year. The new calendar, called the Julian Calendar after him, began on January 1st 45 BC. Although some changes were made to the Julian Calendar by Pope Gregory XIII in 1582, the Roman calendar is still the one we base our calendar on today.

Roman months were *Januarius*—named after Janus the god of beginnings; *Februarius*—from the word meaning 'to clean ceremonially'; *Martialis*—after the god of war, Mars; *Aprilis*—from the word meaning 'opening of flowers'; *Maius*—a month sacred to the goddess of warm weather, Maia; *Junius*—the month of the goddess Juno; *Julius*—originally called Quintilis, the fifth month, but renamed in honour of Julius Caesar; *Augustus*—once called Sextilis, the sixth month, but renamed after the Emperor Augustus. You can work out what *September, October, November* and *December* mean by looking at these Roman numbers:

1	I	uno	6	VI	sex
2	II	duo	7	VII	septem
3	III	tres	8	VIII	octo
4	IIII or IV	quattuor	9	IX	novem
5	V	quinque	10	X	decem

Today we use the Jewish seven-day week but the Romans had an eight-day week. They divided it into seven working days and one (the last one) a market day.

LOOKING FURTHER

You will not have to go very far to find more *evidence* yourself for the Romans in their Empire – now Europe and the Middle East. A good place to start is in a museum. The museum might have Roman objects on display – perhaps mosaics, tombstones or pottery. If the museum near you does not have a Roman collection, the curator will probably be able to tell you where your nearest 'Roman' museum is. From there you might go in search of the *evidence* in towns or in the country-side – look out for town walls, villas, roads or amphitheatres. There is a good guide to remains in Britain: *Roman remains in Britain* by Roger Wilson (Constable) 1980.

Please don't go treasure hunting (especially with a metal detector) like those *clandestini* in Italy (see page 15). Treasure hunters do not care about the past, only the objects they dig up. They often dig into archaelogical sites (even those protected by law) and destroy valuable *evidence*. If you are interested in finding out more about archaeology you could join a national club for young people called the *Young Archaeologists Club*. Write to Kate Pretty, New Hall, Cambridge CB3 0DF for more information.

BIBLIOGRAPHY

Here are some reference books you might find useful if you want to investigate any topic in more detail:

Imperial Rome by Alan Sorrell and Anthony Birley (Lutterworth) 1970
City: A Story of Roman Planning and Construction by David Macauley (Collins) 1975
Town Life in Roman Britain by Mike Corbishley (Harrap) 1981
The Roman Army by Peter Connolly (Macdonald) 1975
Hannibal and the Enemies of Rome by Peter Connolly (Macdonald) 1978
Roman Forts by Roger Wilson (Constable) 1980
Roman Britain – Life in an Imperial Province by Keith Branigan (Readers Digest) 1980

Food and Cooking in Roman Britain by Jane Renfrew (English Heritage) 1985
Apicius: The Roman Cookery Book edited by Barbara Flower and Elizabeth Rosenbaum (Harrap) 1958 – this book has all Apicius' recipes, in Latin and in English.

You might like to read more from the Roman writers you have come across in this book. You will easily find the more famous ones translated in the Penguin Books series. In particular you could read the rest of the play of Plautus:
Plautus: The Rope and other plays translated by E. F. Watling (Penguin) 1964

A good way to find out how the Romans lived is to read stories about them. Here are some you might try:

I marched with Hannibal by Hans Baumann (Oxford) 1961
Eagle in the Snow by Wallace Breem (Gollancz) 1970 – a Roman legion on the German frontier.
The Challenge by Poul Eric Knudsen (Methuen) 1962 – about a Danish charioteer in Rome.
Beyond the Desert Gate by Mary Ray (Faber) 1977 – about the eastern borders of the Roman Empire.
The Ides of April by Mary Ray (Faber) 1971 – murder and mystery in the time of Nero.
Spring Tide by Mary Ray (Faber) 1969 – at the Roman garrison in South Wales.
Outcast by Rosemary Sutcliff (Oxford or Puffin) 1955 – with the Roman surveyors in Kent.
Legions of the Eagle by Henry Treece (Bodley Head or Puffin) 1954 – the Claudian invasion of Britain.
To Spare the Conquered by Stephanie Plowman (Methuen or Penguin) 1960—Queen Boudica leads the struggle against the Roman occupation of Britain.
Song for a Dark Queen by Rosemary Sutcliff (Pelham or Knight) 1978 – an exciting story about Queen Boudica.
The Eagle of the Ninth by Rosemary Sutcliff (Oxford or Puffin) 1954 – follows the Ninth Legion in Britain.

INDEX

Note: page numbers in *italics* refer to illustrations.

A

Actium, battle of 33
actors 58–59, *58*, *61*
aediles 18, 30
Aeneas 17
Aequi 22, 23
aerial photography 11, *10*
Africa 24, 25, 89
Alexandria 7, 31, 33
Alps 22, 25, *26–27*
amphitheatre 9, *9*, 42, 44, *47*, *49*, 54–55, *55*
Amphitheatrum Flavium *see* Colosseum
amphora 44, *44*, 79
animals (wild) 54–55, *55*
antiquaries 10, 11
Antony, Mark 21, 32, 33
Aphrodite 17
Apicius, Marcus 75
apodyterium 53
Apollo 33, *33*, 48
aqueduct 6, *6*, 34, 50
archaeology 12, 13, *13*, 42, 47
arena 54
Aristides, Aelius 44
armour 20, 23, *23*, *26–27*, *30*, *33*, *38–39*, 40, *40*, 54, *54–55*
atrium 14, 72
augur 32, *32*
Augustus (Emperor) 21, 29, 31, 32–33, *32*, *33*, 34, 35, 57
Aurelius, Marcus (Emperor) 62, *62*
Aventine Hill 16

B

bakers, bakery 46, *46*, 77, *77*, *79*
ballista 20, *20*, 42
barracks 41, *41*, 88
basilica 12, *13*, 36, *37*, 48, *49*, 88
Bath 62
baths 52–53, *52–53*, 88
battering rams 20, 38, 42

betting 56
bier 65, *65*
blacksmith 81, *81*
bread 46, *46*, 47, 77
Britain 6, 30, 35, 38, 44, 54, *55*, 86, 89
Brutus, Marcus 31, 32
builders 81, *81*
bulla 67
burial 15, 64–65, *65*, 88
Byzantium 35

C

Caelian hill 16
Caesar, Julius 14, 19, 29, 30–31, *30*, 32, 33, 34, 36, 83, 91
caldarium 52, 53
calendar 91
Caligula (Emperor) 34, 35, 51
camps 39, 40, 42, *43*
Cannae, battle of 25
Capitoline Hill 16, 22
Carthage 25, *25*
Carthaginians 16, 20, 23, *23*, 24, 25, *26–27*, *26–27*, 35
Cassius, Gaius 31, 32
castellum aquae 49, 50
catacombs 63
Cato, Marcus 86, 87
Catullus 64
cavalry 20, 38, 39
cena 74
censors 18, 36
centuriae 20, 38, 39
centurions 20, 21, 38, 39, 41
chariot racing *15*, *16*, *33*, 56–57, *56–57*
children 67, 68–69
Christianity 19, 35, 62, 63, 89
Cicero, Marcus 29, *29*, 30, 55
Circus Maximus 57, *57*
citizens 19, 20, 38
civil war 28, 29, 31, 33
Claudius (Emperor) 18, 20, 34, 35, *35*
Cleopatra 21, 31, 33
clothes 40, *10*, 64, 66, 67, 70 71, *70–71*
cohorts 38
coins 16, *16*, 34, 89
Colchester 54, 63, 68
colonia 48

Colosseum 54–55, *55*
Columella, Lucius 84, 86
comitia 18, 19
comitium 48, 49
Constantine I (Emperor) 35, *35*, 63, 88
Constantinople 35, 88
consuls 18, 19, 20, 28, 30, 34
cooking 74–75, 86
costume, theatrical 58, *58*, *61*
crane 51, *51*
Crassus, Marcus 29
crop-marks *10*, 11
culina 73, 79
curator aquarum 50
curia 19, *19*

D

dates 19, 91
democracy 19
dice 52, 68, *68*
dictator 18, 31
Diocletian (Emperor) 88
dogs 46, *46*, 68, 69, 72, *83*
dole 44
dormice 75
Druids 62

E

education 19, 67, 69
Egypt 29, 33, 34, 44, 67, 71, 89
El Djem 9
elephants 22, *22*, 25, 26, *26–27*, 44, 55
Emperors 6, 9, 18, 20, 21, 32, *32*, 33, 34, 35, *35*, 39, 42, 44, 46, 48, 55, 57, 59, 62, *62*, 63, 88, 89
Empire 32–45, *45*, 88–89
equites 19, 32
Esquiline Hill 16
Etruscans 14–15, *14–15*, 16, 17, 22, 35, 48
excavation 8, 12, 13, *13*

F

factories 80
family 63, 66–67
farming 28, 44, 84–87, *84–87*
fasces 16, 18
fieldwalking 11, *11*

93